Five Eyes on the Fence

Five Eyes on the Fence

Protecting the Five Core Capitals of Your Business

Tony A. Rose

BEP BUSINESS EXPERT PRESS

First published in 2014 by
Business Expert Press, LLC
222 East 46th Street, New York, NY 10017
www.businessexpertpress.com

ISBN-13: 978-1-63157-039-1 (paperback)
ISBN-13: 978-1-63157-040-7 (e-book)

Business Expert Press Entrepreneurship and Small Business Management Collection

Collection ISSN: 1946-5637 (print)
Collection ISSN: 1946-5645 (electronic)

Cover and interior design by Exeter Premedia Services Private Ltd., Chennai, India

First edition: 2014

10 9 8 7 6 5 4 3 2 1

Printed in the United States of America.

To business owners everywhere—who are, by my assessment, heroes.
And, specifically, to my clients, who have allowed me the time,
the insight, and the resources to evaluate the five core capitals.

Abstract

Five Eyes on the Fence: Protecting the Five Core Capitals of Your Business debunks the myth that a business's health is judged by its bottom line alone—by its financial capital. Instead, the book proves that financial capital is a byproduct of four other capitals: (1) *human capital*, defined by a company's and its employees' soft and ingrained attributes like personalities, intelligences, behavioral traits, values, attributes, and motivators; (2) *intellectual capital*, defined by the company's and its employees' knowledge and experience; (3) *social capital*, or the company's network of people and associates; and (4) *structural capital*, the glue that holds all of these capitals together in the form of processes, systems, and modes of delivering a product or service.

When these capitals are combined, a business can create a pixie dust of sorts, allowing its financial capital to grow and thrive.

By exploring both positive and negative case studies, readers learn to consider these five capitals as an intricate web, making decisions according to the interplay between each of the capitals rather than focusing all of their energies on the cold, hard, and logic-driven financial statement.

Keywords

conation, financial capital, human capital, innovative business management, intellectual capital, multiple intelligences in business, social capital, strategic advantage, structural capital, value-based business

Contents

Acknowledgments

It's always hard to pinpoint the exact germination of a business idea because by their very nature entrepreneurs are always looking for new and upgraded ideas. They read, they take classes, they talk to their colleagues. They take one person's idea, combine it with another person's idea, and put a new spin on it. So putting my name on the cover of this book seems a little disingenuous. I would never have started to think about the five core capitals if people before me didn't plant seeds in my mind.

Ronald J. Baker and Paul Dunn wrote *The Firm of the Future*, which is the definitive description of the business of accounting. Baker and Dunn introduced me to the concept of structural capital, and the importance of a multidimensional network of social capital. My friends Mark Wayman, Brian Callahan, and Clara Mayer put the power of relationships into action every day, and they therefore have gobs of social capital.

Then there is the USC Leventhal School of Accounting and Otis College of Art and Design, whose students graciously allowed me to stand before them and discuss human capital, refining my thoughts along the way.

My clients, who shall remain nameless, have discussed the concepts of human, intellectual, social, and structural capital with me over the years. In their quest for greater understanding and self-awareness, they motivated me to think and learn more about the relationships of those four capitals to financial capital.

In my business, I used the principles I learned from Scott Fithian and Todd Fithian of The Legacy Network and Gino Wickman of EOS Worldwide every single day. They generously allowed me to use their intellectual capital in this book as well, as did Kathy Kolbe and the terrific folks at Kolbe Corp, who helped me understand my striving instincts.

It should be noted that this and my first book, *Say Hello to the Elephants*, would not exist unless Dan Sullivan of Strategic Coach encouraged them. Dan's tools, which he generously makes available for entrepreneurs to use in their own businesses, make incalculable differences in their lives and businesses.

And where would I be without David Harper's Vistage Group 2 or my friends at Business Forums International, who gave me a ton of honest feedback and helped me fill in some of my own gaps in knowledge?

Jocelyn Baker is a fine editor and a superhero when it comes to simplifying and organizing my divergent brain. And Michelle Spaulding, researcher extraordinaire, comforted the fact finder in me. Every time she sent me new research, I called Jocelyn and said, "Did you see what Michelle sent? Isn't it great?"

Tim Belber, C. C. Chapman, Curtis Estes, Mary Myers Kauppila, David Kolbe, Jennifer Kushell, Jeffrey Lauterbach, Michael Levin, Ken Merchant, George Myers, John White, Joan Wright, and Art Zaske graciously took the time to read and comment on drafts of this book. I cannot fathom how any of them had any time to give, but I am honored that they chose to devote hours of their lives to me.

And finally, my business partners, my kids, and my wife all deserve medals for bearing with me through this process a second time.

INTRODUCTION

Minding Your Business: The Four Missing Pieces

When I sat down to write this book, I created a timeline. With one book, *Say Hello to the Elephants*, already under my belt, I figured I could definitely write this second book in 90 days. To give myself a little room for rewrites and unexpected obstacles, I padded my internal deadline and gave myself four whole months.

I'm a seasoned pro, I reckoned. Plus, my new book would be straightforward and linear. Four months was aggressive but realistic. It would push me and hold me accountable, but it was definitely doable.

The joke was on me.

Fortunately, my naïvety is your win.

The idea for this book began when one of my new clients, a business that previously failed to file a few forms related to its foreign accounts, was hit with a $3 million tax fine.[1] I assumed that this family-owned business had hired my firm in hopes that I could reduce this $3 million fine as much as possible.

You can imagine my surprise when the CEO made a suggestion during our first meeting: "Why don't we just pay the fine?"

To her, the meeting about a $3 million fine seemed trivial.

To an accountant, though, this suggestion was shocking. Just pay the $3 million fine? The tax code is about 5,000 pages long and jam-packed with intricate loopholes that we accountants spend years studying. What certified public accountant would ever advise his clients to just pay a fine that was in the millions?

I tried to convince the CEO that the meeting was imperative so that we could identify the loopholes that would allow the business to avoid much of the fine and protect its capital.

"That sounds complicated," she said.

She was right. It was not going to be the easiest solution to implement.

"We have plenty of money coming in," she reiterated. "I think we should just pay the fine."

After careful consideration, this is exactly what I recommended.

As I spoke with the CEO, I began seeing that all the energy spent on avoiding the tax would prevent the company from spending its time elsewhere. More than that, because the CEO and the president both valued freedom, the entire environment of the office would be compromised if they felt they were being held captive by a lengthy tax dispute.

"Listen, we got fined, and we learned a lesson," the CEO told me. "We have hired you because we have learned from our mistakes and we do not want to repeat them again. Thanks to your expertise, we will never be hit with a tax fine again, so while paying it does hurt, it will hurt a lot more if we spend our time fighting it."

As I spoke with the CEO, I began to think more clearly about the different components that factor into a business's true health. This company was doing well by financial standards, and aside from its books, I saw other signs of its flourishing health everywhere. The company's employees were engaged and loyal. Customers were lining up to take advantage of its services, which had a rock-solid reputation for excellence. As I mentioned, its financial health was also strong. The company was doing well enough to absorb a $3 million fine (as strange as that might sound).

Now, most of my clients would want to fight the fine, and I would push them to do so. But my encounter with this new client got me thinking about the true signs that denote a company's health.

Most business owners judge their health by financial capital. They treat their financial statements as giant puzzles, hoping to find the perfect balance between trimming overhead and increasing capacity enough to max-out profitability.

They spend their entire careers focused on numbers, but this focus never seems to be enough.

Therein lies the problem: If a company places its primary focus on the bottom line, its long-term success—financial and otherwise—will be compromised, which we saw in the financial crisis of 2008. In fact, financial capital is a *byproduct* of four other types of capital, at least one of which is often entirely ignored.

When a business focuses all of its energies on the cold, hard, and logic-driven financial statement, it is making a critical oversight because the business model does not take into account the softer, other nonmonetary, and often emotion-driven issues that emerge for every buyer.

To be sure, regardless of what kind of industry you are in, your customers' buying decisions are based in large part on their emotions. If you are in the service industry, your customers choose to work with you because they like you, they trust you, and they *feel* that you are reliable, experienced, or credible. Even if you sell generic office supplies, your clients choose your products over all the other generic office supply stores for some emotion-based reasons. Perhaps they believe your product is superior, and that makes them feel as though their clients will consider them to be more impressive. If they are on a budget, your products might make them feel safe because they are inexpensive but of high quality. In one form or another, emotions will always come into play.

This presents a problem for business owners, who are taught to watch the numbers, study the bottom line, and focus on the money. While money will solve all problems that aren't emotional, almost all problems *are* emotional.

Money can be part of the fix, but it is seldom the fix in and of itself.

Have you ever known a person whose only object is to make money? I bet you have. Consider how you feel about that person. The feeling isn't pretty, is it? That person likely uses you (and everyone else) for his or her end game. You needn't spend much time with such a person before realizing that you would rather spend your time with people who display more heart. It is difficult, if not impossible, to have a relationship with a person who considers money as the end-all and be-all.

As the old adage goes: More money will only make you more of what you already are. Individuals who focus primarily on money generally do not have rich values. They might be highly educated or have the ability to impress you with their knowledge, but at best, they will come across as pedantic, elitist, jerks. They care not about you, but about what you bring to the table in terms of helping them reach their financial goals.

The same goes for businesses. Corporate greed is part of the American vernacular because of the perception that too many businesses focus too much on finances.

Although businesses are not supposed to focus all their energies on the bottom line, they need a healthy bottom line to survive. What should they focus on?

Five Eyes on the Fence considers a business's health by looking at five different areas that play a part in determining whether a business has that pixie dust that allows it to succeed and thrive. Indeed, *Five Eyes on the Fence* will prove that financial capital is the byproduct of four other capitals: human, social, structural, and intellectual. Everywhere, businesses are flat-out failing, or at least failing to thrive, because they are keeping only one eye on the fence. They are watching financial capital, and wondering all along why it is not growing faster.

Arguably the most important of all of these capitals is a company's *human capital*, which consists of the company's values and attributes, as well as the values and attributes each employee and executive brings to his or her job. Unlike *intellectual capital*, which consists of companies' or employees' acquired skills, knowledge, and expertise, human capital consists of softer and more ingrained attributes, such as personalities, behavioral traits, values, motivators, and instincts.

Where intellectual capital consists of *what* the company *knows*, human capital consists of *who* the company *is*.

Although others describe the individual human beings who work within a company as human capital, I use the term *social capital* to describe not just the people who work at a company, but also all of the people a company serves, all of the people known by the key employees and executives of a company, and all of the people who serve the company. Your company's social capital represents your network of people and associations.

Finally, and most often ignored, is a business's *structural capital*. We all have ways of doing things. On the personal side, we all have our own unique way of brushing our teeth. You might brush both sides of the lower right quadrant first, while your spouse brushes the front of the bottom teeth first. Businesses also have structural capital in the form of the processes, systems, and modes of delivering a product or service. If a business has great human, intellectual, and social capital, all of which could feed into the financial capital, but the business lacks the systems and protocol to integrate these various capitals, will it ever be financially solvent?

Nope.

And this is why structural capital is necessary.

The interrelationship between all five capitals within a company is the recipe for creating success and the method for innovating solutions. To enjoy any lasting success, a company must have at least one or two other capitals supporting its financial capital, or the company will not be sustainable.

Take, for instance, my client with the $3 million problem. One of the CEO's top values is having a stress-free life, and this attitude is reflected in the company's atmosphere. Employees often arrive at 9:00 or 9:30 a.m. after dropping their children off at school. As long as they are performing at high levels, employees can come and go with little supervision. Children are often seen in the office, playing with office supplies, watching movies on their parents' iPads, or building forts out of boxes. I have even seen employees crawling around in the cardboard-box forts with their children.

What I now know is that when the CEO and her brother were children, their father neglected his family because he was so busy building the very business that his adult children now own. When dad exited the businesses and his daughter and son stepped forward, his children vowed to reverse the trend. While they appreciate everything their father sacrificed to build the business, they believe (and their father agrees) that the best way to honor all of those years of hard work and sacrifice is to put their families first.

As a result, the company places a tremendous amount of emphasis on human and social capital. It has done a remarkable job of identifying the behavioral traits and skill sets of employees who work well in a loosely regulated environment. Every single employee—including the mailroom clerk, receptionists, and part-time staff members—has been handpicked by the best human resources director I have ever met. When it comes to hiring employees who will over deliver in a relaxed environment, she is part behavioral psychologist and part magician. Rarely does the company need to let someone go, and when it does, the termination is done kindly, promptly, and usually within a few weeks of the person being hired.

Likewise, the company has developed deep and familial roots with its clients. From what I gather, the relationship between the company and its clients is truly mutually beneficial, with both sides thinking they have the better end of the deal. As a result, the clients overlook the company's informalities, and most of them even embrace it. The employees socialize with clients. Clients know employees' spouses and children. Clients and employees are invited to respective holiday parties.

All of these relationships have been developed through a strong emphasis on human and social capital, so as I evaluated the CEO's request to just pay the $3 million fine, I began seeing the wisdom of her position.

To lower the fine, she would have had to spend many hours in tax litigation. These hours would take her away from the business during the day, which meant she would have to work in the evenings and on the weekends, when she should have been spending time with her family.

Beyond that, the process was going to take a long time. Without a guarantee of the outcome, the company would be unable to evaluate its actual financial health and make strategic decisions accordingly. The company would be in limbo for months, if not years.

This would not fare well for a company that valued a relaxed environment, above all else. In fact, by focusing too much on financial capital, the company would probably erode the culture that allowed its financial capital to thrive.

Still, it was painful for me as an accountant to watch my client hand money to the IRS, so I pushed back a little bit, explaining that a few strategies were guaranteed to work and therefore would not add any pressure to the company. The CEO and CFO agreed that I could apply any techniques that were no-brainers but forego strategies that would require extended negotiations.

They wanted to pay attention to the financial capital, but within the context of the entire organization, its culture, and its values.

The truth was that the company *did* have plenty of money coming in. Although most companies would balk at such a large fine, this company was able to arrange a payment plan that allowed it to absorb the fine over a matter of several years. It was the best solution for the company, its clients, its employees, and their families. I believe that its bottom line was probably better in the long run because it made this decision.

If this company is able to thrive by adding just human and social capital to the mix, imagine the strength of its financial capital due to the combined forces of its rich and strong set of values (human capital), great relationships (social capital), and knowledge that people want (intellectual capital), all of which are integrated into efficient, process-oriented systems (structural capital)?

Why, of course, the financial capital takes care of itself!

When a company is able to offer all of these capitals, it feels wealthier, is wealthier, and has more to offer to its clients. It also has a financial tarp that allows it to grow as well as weather storms created by internal or external forces.

During my earliest musings, I had seen this book as neatly defined—something I could deliver in a package that was clearly organized, linear, and ready for action. When examining the five different capitals of a business, I imagined that I would write about each of the five capitals in five cleanly delineated chapters that I could wrap neatly with a bow. Then I would tie the book up with a conclusion, and send my book off to the publishers.

I was wrong. In fact, as you will come to see, I was ridiculously naïve.

While it is true that each of the five capitals have some unique characteristic, they are inextricably tangled within a company in the same way that a person's behavioral traits are woven together to create a human being. Can you extract your values from your social network? Of course not. Your closest network of friends has been chosen by your value system, and your values have likely changed based on input from your friends, colleagues, and associates within your social capital network.

Likewise, your intellectual capital has grown, changed, and been influenced by the people in your life and the values that motivate you to take action and grow your mind.

And just like a person who has compromised his or her values (human capital) can create a tangled web of lies that ends in financial repercussions like divorce, a business's flawed values could affect relationships with customers (social capital), thereby harming its financial capital.

I should have known that writing this book, then, would be much more complicated than allotted for in my four-month time frame, but our minds tend to try and compartmentalize things so that we can understand them a little bit at a time.

It's only when we have a deep, intimate understanding that we can start seeing the subtle intricacies among all the capitals. Now, over 16 months later, I embrace the notion that the examination of all the capitals that go into a business is not as easy as I had originally thought. Just as a thriving business is exponentially harder to maintain than one that is just okay, the capitals are not as neatly severable as I had assumed. There is a magic—I call it pixie dust—that goes into examining and integrating the different capitals. This may be why there are no other books that examine and integrate all five capitals (that I know of).

A company is benefited with certain grandeur in having a big, complicated web of integrated capitals. When it makes a small shift to improve a structural capital, for instance, it could be strikingly more attractive from a social capital perspective.

To be sure, though, and as a result of the complex relationship between all the capitals, this book is not comprehensive—not by any means. It is the beginning examination of the relationship between the five factors that define the success of your business. This book alone will not solve all of your business's problems, nor will it provide a crisp diagram from which you can replicate processes to create the perfect business.

It is my hope that you begin to take notice of five capitals and how they relate to one another within the fences surrounding your business so that you can say: *That makes sense. I'm going to direct my attention there and take a deeper look.*

The truth is: The magic of integrating the capitals lies in the hands of the owners. Without knowing your values, your networks, your product, and your systems, I cannot give you the exact formula. I can hand you a few tools, but you are the artist.

As you begin examining the webbed and linked fence of your business, notice the subtle intricacies. Decisions you make on a day-to-day basis will more likely than not have influence on more capitals than you think. Notice that the magic is not in perfecting the balance sheet but rather in honoring all five of the core components of your business.

The Capitals and Me

While this book is specifically for entrepreneurs and business owners, the first step toward understanding and integrating these different types of capital is identifying your own personal resources in terms of human, intellectual, social, structural, and financial capital. Only once you understand your personal resources and how you, as an individual integrate them, can you apply this information to the approaches you use with your clients, employees, friends, family members, or vendors.

In this way, this book pertains to anyone—from college student to retiree. If you are a non-business owner reading this book, the principles will remain relevant to you as an individual. Throughout, you will notice boxes titled "The Capitals and Me." Rather than being directed to a business owner, this information is specific to an individual qua individual, so be on the lookout!

CHAPTER 1

Human Capital

Who you are as a person is of great worth. Not only do you have certain intelligences, such as musical, mathematical, or linguistic intelligences, but you also have values, such as kindness, generosity, thriftiness, or directness.

You also have an internal wiring that defines how you act with your values and intelligences as a context and motivator. When faced with a task or a goal, how do you look as you go about attaining success? What is your first instinct? Do you seek information? Do you create a model? Do you create a system? Do you just jump in the water and swim?

This internal wiring is called *conation*, or *striving instincts*.

Together, intelligences, values, and conation create the essence of you as a person. Where intelligence is the material of your behavior, values are the soil from which your behaviors grow, and conation is the method by which you naturally express these values and intelligences.

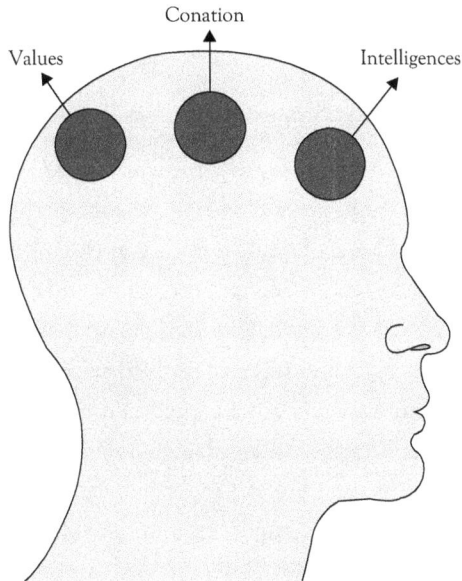

Human capital, then, is defined by the depth of your intelligence, the richness of your values, and the focus of your conative energies. Within an organization, human capital can be considered both individually and holistically to answer the following questions:

- Are the right employees working in the right roles?
- Are we tapping into the motivations of our employees and creating an environment that naturally drives them to produce?
- Are we honoring our employees' values, and are they honoring the company's values?
- Are we identifying the depth of our employees' skills and then allocating their unique abilities appropriately?

Before we look at the role of human capital in an organization, though, let's break this puzzle apart to consider the three components of human capital:

1. Intelligences
2. Values
3. Conation

The First Component of Human Capital: Intelligences

Have you noticed that the word *intelligences* is plural? This is because there is no such thing as being intelligent and being unintelligent. (When used to describe a person, I always say that the word *stupid* is just plain stupid.)

All of us have multiple intelligences, a concept that was best considered by Harvard psychologist Howard Gardner in his book *Multiple Intelligences*. A person could be intelligent in his or her capacity to think in musical notes, hear patterns, and manipulate them. He or she might also have the ability to solve physical problems. This same person might lack the ability to understand other people, and he or she might not have strong verbal skills. Despite the fact that an individual's interpersonal and verbal skills are not as great as another person's, he or she still has multiple intelligences that are equally important and valuable when applied to the right setting.

Gardner identified the following intelligences:

- Verbal or linguistic: A person with verbal or linguistic intelligence is articulate and has the ability to use words to make himself or herself be understand, and to describe others.
- Logical or mathematical: This person can spot the fundamentals behind cause-and-effect systems and excels at math, logic games, and puzzles.
- Visual or spatial: A person with a visual or spatial intelligence is aware of his or her environment, can visualize this environment internally, and can therefore navigate and solve spatial problems.
- Musical or rhythmic: This person can truly hear music. This includes rhythms, tone, pitch, patterns, and the interrelationship between these elements.
- Bodily or kinesthetic: A person with a bodily or kinesthetic intelligence has a high degree of control of his or her body, and a corresponding awareness of his or her body or a body part.
- Naturalist: A naturalist is in tune with his or her surroundings, which include plants, animals, minerals, weather, geographical formations, and other natural elements.
- Intrapersonal: This person is highly self-aware and understands his or her own strengths, weaknesses, motivations, and abilities.
- Interpersonal: A person with interpersonal intelligence has the ability to understand other people's strengths, weaknesses, motivations, and abilities. This person is highly empathetic.
- Existential: This person is adept at posing questions and formulating theories about life, death, and the metaphysical world.

These are the intelligences that Gardner identified, but I suspect there are others that do not fit neatly into any of his categories. A friend of mine is a simplifier. She takes all sorts of information—verbal, written, physical, or numeric—and puts it in order. She makes sense of things, which seemingly puts her in the logical or mathematical category, but this is too narrow of a view. In addition to being a whiz with numbers, she can clarify miscommunications or extract and reiterate the germane information from a tangential conversation with a client.

For her, I would like to add the category of simplifier, and I'm sure there are many others to be added as well, but they probably would not meet all of the criteria that Professor Gardner outlines in defining an intelligence.

It bears noting that Professor Gardner has not identified any precise instruments for measuring whom has which intelligence or intelligences. Rather, an intelligence is sensed. Some are easy to define, and if you have ever watched me play golf or shoot hoops, you would know that it is often easy to spot when a person does *not* have a certain intelligence.

Sadly, as a culture, we primarily recognize people with verbal, linguistic, logical, and mathematical intelligences. Scholastic aptitude tests and IQ tests look only at these traditional intelligences. We say that people who have musical skills are talented. We degrade manual laborers, as though their bodily or kinesthetic intelligence is less important than those who do well on standardized tests. A charming person who is good with people might, in fact, be an interpersonal genius with as much importance as a scientist or a professor of fine literature.

The point, here, is that if we continue to confine the word intelligence to only verbal, linguistic, mathematic, and logical skills, we might miss seeing and appreciating the intelligences of those around us. A person might not be the sharpest tack when it comes to verbal and logical intelligences, but that same person might be able to see patterns in ways that can arrange offices for greatest productivity, or be able to fix things with the use of his or her hands, or have incredible empathy in his or her dealings with others.

Each of these intelligences can be brought to great use in organizations.

One of my colleagues told me about her customer service employees: Becca and Kathy. Becca is the more articulate of the two. When customers need information about the product, Becca is the go-to person, and because she has a greater ability to relay information, she can move through calls much faster than Kathy. At first glance, Becca seems like the star of the show.

On closer look, one sees that Kathy offers something that Becca lacks. When an angry customer calls the support line, the calls are always directed to Kathy, who has managed to help the company repair the damage with more than a few angry customers. During the frenzied holiday seasons, when complaints skyrocket, Kathy is the star of the show. When a nit-picky client calls with a seemingly irrelevant but time-consuming complaint, Kathy remains pleasant, unruffled, and helpful.

Whereas Becca has more in the way of verbal and linguistic intelligence, Kathy's interpersonal intelligence is off the charts. She is empathetic, loving, and has the ability to always see the other person's perspective. Fortunately, her employers do not pressure her to be something that she is not. They recognize that Kathy plays an important position on the team, and they direct appropriate assignments to her. Under a traditional definition, Becca is the smarter employee. With a stronger grasp of language, Becca simply presents herself as much more articulate, and she is the person most companies would hire. To be sure, Becca is the go-to person in most cases. But my colleague knows that while Becca upholds the company's brand, Kathy has an interpersonal intelligence that makes her just as valuable as Becca because of her role in client retention.

To be certain, one person's intelligences—whatever they are—are just as important and just as valuable as the next, but this alone does not define the richness of a person's human capital. Consider, for instance, that both author John Steinbeck and Nazi propagandist Josef Goebbels

The Capitals and Me

Identifying your specific intelligences is important, and so too is identifying the intelligences you *do not* possess. In doing so, you will begin to appreciate the people in your life who exhibit different intelligences. The next time you start thinking that a person in your life is stupid, remind yourself that you lack intelligence in some of the nine areas.

To hone in on your intelligences, you might want to circle the intelligences you possess, as well as those you do not possess:

Intelligences I Possess	Intelligences I Do Not Possess
Verbal and linguistic	Verbal and linguistic
Logical and mathematical	Logical and mathematical
Visual and spatial	Visual and spatial
Musical and rhythmic	Musical and rhythmic
Bodily and kinesthetic	Bodily and kinesthetic
Naturalist	Naturalist
Intrapersonal	Intrapersonal
Interpersonal	Interpersonal
Existential	Existential

had incredible linguistic and interpersonal intelligences. Why was the effect they had on the world and society so stunningly different?

It has to do with the second component of human capital: values.

The Second Component of Human Capital: Values

Steinbeck and Goebbels had opposing methods of deploying their intelligence: Steinbeck, through the gentler values of inspiration, kindness, and art; and Goebbels, through ruthless and destructive values.

We are able to determine a lot about the richness of people or organizations by taking a look at how their values direct their intelligences. If a company values only money, it may throw ethics to the side and align itself with the Bernie Madoffs of the world. A company that values aesthetics might emerge alongside companies like Anthropologie and Apple.

Your values, whatever they are, define how you express your intelligences. Although a value system can be objectively wrong—as in the case of Goebbels—most value sets are neither right nor wrong. Rather, they represent a combination of that which is passed on from prior generations, your aspirations, and the stage of your life.

1. The first set of values generally manifest as attributes. That is, either you are born with them or they are instilled at such an early age

that they are practically hardwired into your being. These values are seemingly passed on genetically, or they are nurtured into you. If your parents were philanthropic, if they loved to be outside, and if they loved to argue about politics at the dinner table, you likely carry a set of values that includes generosity, an active lifestyle, and a similar political leaning or set of ethics. This explains why most children belong to the same religion and political party as their parents.

2. While some values are attributes, others are motivators. You might want to be something that you have never had. If your family declared bankruptcy twice and you never felt financially secure, you might find security in your top five values. If you have never felt physically healthy, you might value clean living more than someone who has enjoyed good health her entire life. If your parents divorced when you were too young to remember, you might hold intimacy as an aspirational value.

3. Finally, some values also move up and down the scale of priorities based on the stage of your life. These values can be attributes or motivators, but what makes them unique is that they move up and down in importance based specifically on the stage of your life. If you are a parent, you might say that your family is one of your core values, whereas it might not be in the top five if you are nineteen years old. If you are nearing retirement, you might value leisure and hobbies more than you did when you were just starting your business.

Regardless, if your values are positive values, they all have a place in a business, and they are neither right nor wrong. A person who values kindness and patience might be great at managing accounts with difficult clients, particularly if that person has an intelligence in interpersonal dynamics. A direct and frugal person who is highly intelligent in mathematics and logistical abilities would serve an accounts receivable department well. Good values will help countless teams—personal or professional—reach goals.

We all have values, but failing to identify them stops us from leveraging them to their fullest extent. By recognizing and naming these values, we are able to make decisions that better reinforce and honor them. An awareness of values provides a context for decision making because every decision is born in a value of some kind. Awareness of what value—positive

The Capitals and Me

Have you ever made a decision that did not resonate with you? Or have you ever said, "I'll do it, but it is against my better judgment!"? Chances are that you are acting in a way that does not honor your core values. Identifying your values puts them at the forefront of your mind, making it easier to recognize and avoid situations that call for you to ignore or dishonor these values.

So the question is: What are your core values?

Look through the following list of values and select the top 15 values that are most important to you. It's a long list, so I suggest that you start by taking a pencil or a pen and drawing a line through those that do not resonate with you. (Note that I had an early childhood value instilled in me by my parents: Never write in a book. When parishioners wrote in their Bibles during church, I thought God was going to swallow them up. So if you are incapable of writing in this book without violating one of your values, grab a notebook by all means!)

Once you have eliminated those values that are not near the top of your list, you will have an easier time narrowing the list down to 15.

And by all means, add any values that you think are missing!

Adventure: Participation in new and exciting experiences.
Community: Cooperating and identifying with others' shared interests.
Courage: Perseverance and bravery and the ability to face difficulties.
Creativity: Imagination, inspiration, and having new and original ideas.
Decisiveness: The ability to make firm and definitive decisions that provide clear direction.
Diversity: Appreciation of individual differences.
Education: Pursuing intellectual endeavors and gaining knowledge.
Enjoyment: Valuing the pursuit of pleasure and delight.
Environment: Valuing nature and the need to care for and live in harmony with our planet.
Ethics: Moral standards and principles of conduct.
Excellence: Achievement of quality and competence in everyday activities.

Faith: Devotion and dedication to a set of beliefs.

Family: To have a happy, loving family.

Freedom: Liberty to act and speak without restriction.

Friendship: To have a network of close and supportive friends.

Fun: Play, laughter, and the ability to be amused.

Giving: Making monetary or time donation to benefit others.

Growth: To keep changing and growing and challenging yourself.

Happiness: Contentment, satisfaction, and fulfillment.

Health: Physical fitness and emotional well-being.

Helpfulness: Desire to aid and assist others.

Honesty: To be truthful and forthright.

Idealism: Striving for perfection.

Independence: To be self-sufficient and free from dependence on others.

Intimacy: Maintaining close and deep relationships.

Justice: To promote fair and equal treatment for every individual.

Knowledge: To learn and contribute valuable knowledge.

Leadership: The ability to motivate others toward the achievement of a goal.

Leisure: Taking time to relax and enjoy life.

Loyalty: Faithful commitment to people and ideals.

Meaningful activity: Pursuits that have purpose and lasting value.

Nurturance: Assisting others in need or hardship and being of service to others.

Optimism: Believing that it will all work out.

Order: To have a life that stays fairly consistent, well-ordered, and organized.

Popularity: To be well liked by many people.

Privacy: Free from intrusion and the right to confidentiality.

Recognition: Being acknowledged and appreciated.

Respect: Ability to demonstrate admiration and esteem toward others.

Security: The safety and comfort that comes from protection and certainty.

Solitude: Tranquility and peace and time to be apart from others.

Spirituality: Desire to understand one's inner soul and relationship with the world.

Teamwork: Working with others to achieve a goal.

Thankfulness: To live in a state of appreciation for the people and things that populate your life.

Trust: To be reliable and dependable.

Truthfulness: Honesty, integrity, and being forthright.

Variety: Embracing unpredictability in life, and the challenges and opportunities that change provides.

Wealth: Security and freedom provided by accumulating assets.

Work: Fulfillment of a duty to achieve a purpose.

List your top 15 values in the following spaces.

1. _____
2. _____
3. _____
4. _____
5. _____
6. _____
7. _____
8. _____
9. _____
10. _____
11. _____
12. _____
13. _____
14. _____
15. _____

Narrow down the top 15 to the top 10 values.

1. _____
2. _____
3. _____
4. _____
5. _____

6. _____

7. _____

8. _____

9. _____

10. _____

Narrow down the top 10 to the top 5 values.

1. _____

2. _____

3. _____

4. _____

5. _____

As you completed this exercise, you likely had several *a-ha!* moments whereby you realized that you unconsciously made certain choices based on your values. A friend of mine values solitude and community above all else. This is an unusual combination that tells me her moods swing wide. She's an extreme extrovert at times, but these gregarious moments are almost always trailed by long period of solitude and introspection.

One of her husband's top values, on the other hand, is intimacy.

"No wonder I get aggravated within three minutes of my husband walking in the door," she told me. "I'm sitting there enjoying my solitude, and he walks in and wants to connect with me immediately. I need a few minutes to make the radical shift from enjoying my alone-time to engaging with my husband."

By gaining clarity on their values, my friend and her husband were able to work together to resolve a source of frustration. Her husband ultimately felt that his value of intimacy was being better served when he helped his wife avoid the frustration associated with interruption of her alone time. It was a small step that made a huge difference.

When my friend identified her values, she made other changes as well. She realized that she previously was making decisions that complicated her life. She joined networking and volunteer groups, committed to participating on committees, and then had a to-do list that was a mile long. While joining networking and volunteer groups honored her value of community, all of the homework prevented her from having enough true solitude. Now she realizes that her top value of community can better support her other top value of solitude if her community engagements are purely social instead of being attached to homework that requires her to sacrifice her solitude. She dropped out of the committees, stopped volunteering, quit her book club, and took ownership of her alone time.

or negative—a pending decision honors can make a person more resolute in that decision, or it can prevent a person from making a huge mistake.

We are also better able to resolve conflict when we realize that our behavior—and the behavior of others—is tied to a value.

Imagine two business partners: Tom values independence, happiness, respect, harmony, and friendship. His partner, Anne, values truth, ethics, education, growth, and wealth. Now imagine that a recession hits. The accounting practice that once had $10 million worth of business now has $8 million worth of business. Anne and Tom must decide between two choices:

- Keep all the employees, and Anne and Tom will earn 30 percent of what they earned the prior year.
- Keep 70 percent of their employees, and Anne and Tom will earn 80 percent of what they earned the prior year.

If it were solely up to Tom, the company would keep all its employees and the partners would draw less salary. If it were up to Anne, the company would let go of nonessential employees so that the partners could pull the largest possible salaries. Without having first identified their values, what is the most likely way Anne and Tom would resolve this conflict?

A fight would ensue, of course. Tom would call Anne heartless and greedy. Anne would tell Tom that he was being a wimp. Then they would argue about who leaves their unwashed coffee mugs in the office sink.

Yet, neither Tom nor Anne is wrong. The value itself is not causing a problem. The problem is that business partners have not agreed on the core values of their enterprise, so each person's respective partner is unable to understand and honor the difference of opinion.

If we take a moment to consider their values, we can see that independence, happiness, respect, harmony, and friendship are important to Tom; truth, ethics, education, growth, and wealth are important to Anne. If they both recognize these values right away, they will have the clarity to accomplish two things. These are the same two things you can do when you identify your values:

1. You are able to explain your behavior or your decisions by citing your value set. When others understand why you choose to behave in certain ways, you are able to avoid conflict or, at a minimum, resolve many conflicts by finding solutions that support both people's values.
2. You are able to shift behavior that does not align with your values. When you make decisions, you can reflect on which choices affirm your top values and which choices betray your top values.
3. When you begin to understand which values are motivating values and which are attributes, you can more easily intentionally act in ways that move you toward those long-term aspirations. Someone who aspires to the values of environment and teamwork might join the Sierra Club.

It's right there in the name: Hardwiring is *hard* to change. Motivation makes it much easier.

The Capitals and Me

Be aware of your own judgments and assumptions. Unless we spend time identifying our own values, and then noticing that other people have equally important values that might differ from ours, we will likely walk into situations with expectations of what we believe is important. Creating great interpersonal solutions requires that you recognize and verbalize your own values, and then leave room for other people to honor their values.

Identifying values also informs a company's intellectual capital, its social capital, and its structural capital. Take a look at Disney Theme Parks.

Since Disneyland opened in 1955, Disney theme parks have been the undisputed industry leader around the world. In 2011, Disney theme parks held the top eight positions in the list of top ten theme parks worldwide by attendance, as published by Themed Entertainment Association. As a group, Disney theme parks attract two and one-half times more visitors than any other entertainment group attracts.

In other words, the company is doing well.

Disneyland's initial success is due in part to the fact that the product was certainly revolutionary in its day. Walt Disney knew he could improve upon the shoddy, ill-kept amusement parks he sometimes visited with his daughters. He had a vision to create a place that parents could enjoy as much as their children, and a simple mission to make people happy.

And Disney had some unique intellectual capital, specifically the talent and ability of movie studio art directors and designers to bring stories to life.

Disney took advantage of unique structure capital as well; the company produced a television show that was leveraged to promote the new theme park.

Yet the company possessed no intellectual or structural capital so proprietary that it could not and has not been imitated. Rival theme parks tell stories, leverage film-studio assets, spend millions on amazing attractions and advertisements. Yet 55 years later, Disney's dominance remains unchallenged.

I submit that it is not intellectual, structural, or social capital that sets Disney apart. It is unique *human capital* that has been applied to the intellectual, structural, and social capital.

Disneyland was founded on two stated values that have stood the test of time: *family* and *happiness*. Additional values have added power and longevity to Disney theme parks. Walt Disney himself possessed almost legendary human capital that was infused into the character and structure of Disneyland. His *optimism* and *idealism* were reflected in Fantasyland, a land section of the Magic Kingdom parks where there can be no cynicism, where dreams come true, good overcomes evil, and the wonder of childhood is preserved. The same optimism is expressed in the adventure, accomplishment, and forward progress celebrated throughout the theme park.

In the first official description of Disneyland, written in 1953, Bill Walsh expressed this human capital beautifully:

Disneyland will be based upon and dedicated to the ideals, the dreams, and hard facts that have created America. And it will be uniquely equipped to dramatize these dreams and facts and send them forth as a source of courage and inspiration to all the world.

Disneyland will be something of a fair, an exhibition, a playground, a community center, a museum of living facts, and a showplace of beauty and magic.

It will be filled with the accomplishments, the joys and hopes of the world we live in. And it will remind us and show us how to make those wonders part of our own lives.

Disneyland was also founded on the values of *respect* for people and a *trust* that if you appeal to people's better nature, they will respond. In reply to fears that Main Street vehicles would be vandalized, Walt Disney is quoted as saying: "Don't worry about it. Just make them beautiful and you'll appeal to the best side of people. They all have it; all you have to do is bring it out."

This is human capital in a nutshell. Visitors to Disney theme parks are treated with respect. They are not referred to as customers or consumers. They are guests. Courtesy is the most emphasized and enduring standard for theme park employees, who are called cast members. They are expected to be helpful, attentive, and friendly, and they consistently rise to that expectation.

Walt Disney was emphatic about cleanliness and believed that a clean environment contributed to happiness. He disliked run-down, trashed amusement parks, and demanded better for Disneyland. Cleanliness may be considered a value, but in the case of Disneyland, it was predicated on the more powerful underlying value of respect: respect for surroundings and respect for others. Walt Disney expected his park to be clean and beautiful because he respected his guests and trusted that they would respect his park. Today, cast members who notice a piece of trash are responsible for picking it up, whether they play the role of custodian or CEO.

Disney theme parks provide an excellent example of the power of human capital and the power of identifying values. Their values aren't just expressed in a document. They are honored in every nook and cranny, vividly displayed in a theme park, a world of its own, built on family, happiness, idealism, optimism, respect, and trust. Disney's human capital is a set of values that have inspired generations of cast members and guests; human capital has kept Disney theme parks the undisputed leaders in the industry.

Important to note is that Disneyland has intentionally identified and used these values to its benefit. Like Disney, many business owners are able to accelerate their success by identifying their values and then strategically building them into the company's behaviors.

Consider, for instance, a client of mine who found himself in a world of hurt 30 years ago. John's top value is *friendship*. I suspect he spends 30 percent of his day writing handwritten notes crafted in beautiful penmanship to the long list of people he loves and who love him. He has nurtured his friendships above all else.

Thirty years ago, when the bank was breathing down his neck and John was about to lose everything he owned, every single person in John's life wanted to see him succeed. Even casual acquaintances could not bear the thought of seeing John's business and livelihood sink.

So they rallied. A business connection called upon an employee who knew a banker who had a customer who stepped forward to buy into John's business, become his partner, and prevent the business from going under.

Thirty years later, this business is thriving with the same partners. Both are wealthier than they would have been without each other. This, all because John had the wisdom to use his unique human capital to let everyone in his network know that he values them as a friend.

The Capitals and Me

Identifying your personal values serves two critical purposes: First, it allows you to identify from where your decisions and core beliefs stem. When you make a decision, you can identify which foundational value (or attribute) you are honoring or, if the decision is a bad decision, violating. The other reason to identify your personal values is to identify those values that motivate you into action, which I call aspirational values. When you identify the top three foundational values (or attributes), as well as the top three aspiring values, you are much more likely to make decisions and act in accordance with your deepest wishes. If your top three aspirational values, for instance, are recognition, leadership, and excellence, you might make a decision to write a column that situates you as a thought leader. If your top three attributes are work, loyalty, and community, you would more easily release an employee who has betrayed you and created a negative work environment.

Keep in mind that a business owner's values and a business's values are not the same thing. Gino Wickman, founder and chief value officer (my title for him, not his) of EOS,[1] has come upon a simple method of helping to identify a company's core values (described on pages 32–33). For now, though, let's focus on what makes a person tick.

The Third Component of Human Capital: Conation

Your conative strength is the third part of your personal human capital. Think of conation like this: If you want to do something (because of your values), and you know how to do it (because of your intelligences), then conation is the way you look when you go about doing it.

Your conation represents your striving instincts, a term coined by Kathy Kolbe, who created the industry standard for measuring conation. To describe conation, I want to start by giving you an example of two people with different striving instincts: Jenn and Carrie.

Over the years, I have had the fortune of working with many different employees and watching their striving instincts play out in an office setting. One of my employees, Jenn, worked for me in the early 2000s. Jenn got things done. If I walked to her desk and asked her to order a new printer for me, she was on Staples' website before I had returned to my desk. She didn't always get me the best deal, but she could mark things off her to-do list like no one's business. Spending an extra $30 on a printer was worth it because Jenn put her own time to such great use.

When Jenn left, she was replaced by Carrie, who ended up being an equally valuable employee, but for different reasons. If I asked Carrie to order a new printer, she would have spent her time finding the right printer at the lowest price. The task would not have been accomplished as quickly as it would have been under Jenn's direction, but when the printer arrived, our office would never have any problems integrating it into our network because it would be the perfect printer. Plus, Carrie would know what kind of ink it needed, she would have ordered the proper stockpile of ink, and because she would read the manual, she could easily trouble-shoot any small problems, should they arise.

Within a company, employees all have individual ways they go about solving problems, getting answers, and expressing their intelligences and their values. Very often, when two people come from different places of acting, they can create conflict, particularly if they do not understand the other person's striving instincts. Although I cannot know for sure, I imagine that Jenn and Carrie would not mesh well if they had both worked on my team at the same time. Carrie would be uncomfortable with Jenn's quick trigger; Jenn would be aggravated by Carrie's thorough and deliberate process.

On the other hand, two people's opposing conative instincts might act as complementary, so long as they are identified up front and under-stood by both parties. Carrie could be grateful that Jenn is the type of person who speeds up the process, and Jenn might be thankful that Carrie acts as a safety net who prevents Jenn from making mistakes that inevita-bly occur when a person acts too quickly.

I call Jenn a quick start and Carrie a fact finder, terms I have taken from Kathy Kolbe. Kathy Kolbe created something called the Kolbe System™ (www.kolbe.com), which determines a person's method of operation or striv-ing instincts. The Kolbe A Index™ looks at the deeply imbedded instincts that determine how you will go about solving problems, making decisions, and taking action. Kolbe segments these characters into four types of energy:

1. Gathers and shares information: fact finder.
2. Arranges and designs solutions: follow through.

3. Deals with risk and uncertainty: quick start.

4. Models or seeks to make the intangible tangible: implementer.

All of us tend to go about solving problems in ways that seem right to them. It seems right because some way, somehow we have a natural neuron string that moves us to a particular style of solving those problems. Like Carrie, I feel most comfortable if I am able to gather facts first. Would I ever buy a printer without researching it first? Sure, but it would never quite feel right, and I would be a lot happier if I knew that my decision was backed by research to support my decision.

Others are bored silly by the fact-finding process. Their mantra? Time is money! They need to jump right in, guess at the solution, and learn by process of trial and error.

Kathy Kolbe proved scientifically that if you are asked or required to act using sets of neurological paths that are less suited to your natural wiring, you will be in a position of strain or stress. She has found that our brains do not operate as efficiently when we are forced to act in ways that do not fit the natural way we get things done. It is a little like trying to write left-handed if you are a righty—you can do it, but it does not work as well, it will not feel right.

Imagine that you are an employee who initiates in quick start but not in fact finding. You like to jump right in and get to work, but you also have low tolerance for fact-finding missions. If your boss requires that you complete heavy research prior to taking an action, you will likely be bored and also exhausted. On the flip side, if you need to find facts before taking action, your heart will start to race when everyone around you is pulling the trigger without gathering all the evidence in advance. You will feel anxiety, and you will always feel a few steps behind.

Consider the implications for a business owner. Imagine that you need an assistant who can initiate and keep working on a myriad of projects all at one time, but your assistant needs to be able to finish things in front of him or her before moving onto the next task.

Your assistant will be under stress, and you might start to believe that he or she is ineffective (and he might be ineffective in this role). If this continues over a long period of time, he or she will not be very productive, and you will be frustrated and dissatisfied.

And this same employee might be a radiantly happy super star if he or she is moved into a data management position.

Before the partners at my firm knew about the Kolbe System, we questioned why certain people who were promoted to supervisor or manager were not as successful as we would have imagined. When we were introduced to the Kolbe System, we began to notice patterns. First, all of the named partners have similar and complementary Kolbe profiles, which means we have naturally banded together to form a certain environment. In fact, all the managers and supervisors who were performing as expected shared Kolbe make-ups that were similar to ours. Almost all of those who were underperforming shared a different Kolbe make-up, which made them great as employees, but not-so-great as leaders in our organization.

Specifically, the managers and supervisors who were underperforming required more time to start a project than we allotted. They were not effective in pulling the trigger quickly, and they had issues with multitasking.

I cannot say which came first: Did we create the environment, or did our Kolbe profiles make us more natural leaders? Regardless, we began changing our language so that these managers and supervisors could perform in our environment. As we all grew more aware of each team member's striving instinct, we were more able to accommodate different work styles, giving managers and supervisors the space to work in alignment with their conative strengths. We trained, supervised, and mentored differently.

The Kolbe System believes, as do I, that much of what we have identified as workplace burnout could well have been a situation where a certain person with a conative construct is put in a position of having to act for a long period of time outside that natural mode of operation. Burnout happens when that person simply has to remove himself or herself to find relief.

Applying Human Capital in a Business Setting

Start your examination of the human capital within your organization by considering three questions:

1. Do you understand your employees and do they understand you?
2. Are you hiring employees in accordance with your values?
3. Do you have the right team members doing the right things?

Respecting the Individual Employees

Plain and simple: Your employees will be unable to sustain a lasting commitment to their jobs if they are required to work in a situation that counters their values, if they fail to have their intelligences recognized and used, and if their unique natural instincts conflict with their tasks.

Many organizations make the mistake of considering one value—hard work—and deciding that this value trumps all else. They take a hard-working employee and shove a pile of work onto her desk, ignoring whether he or she has the intelligences or instincts to sustain this work. Plus, the individual might be hard working, but does he or she have competing values that trump hard work? An employee who has young children or a new spouse might be willing to work hard during office hours, but unwilling to work overtime.

A hard-working employee might value perfection, and an increased and a hurried workload might threaten this value. An employee might be capable of working hard when the task suits his or her intelligences, but he or she might be bored silly, confused, or sloppy when it comes to tasks that fall outside the individual's areas of expertise.

In the long run, it pays to know your employees. You will be more likely to retain staff members for many years if you treat them as unique individuals instead of cogs in a machine. The use of alternative work environments and work schedules, for instance, allows you to retain people of unique constructs and have a greater range of talents in your office. For example, consider employees with young children, who often switch jobs or exit the workforce entirely because long working hours force them to spend too much time away from home. These employees often have robust intellectual capital that adds to a team. If an employer offers them alternate work schedules (in exchange for altered compensation packages), the employees might stay on the team.

In other words, when it comes to employees, one size does not fit all. One size fits one.[2]

Hiring Employees

Gino Wickman is an entrepreneur's entrepreneur. He is, in fact, so betrothed to developing entrepreneurs that he has written four books on the subject, and he has created an entrepreneurial training program called the Entrepreneurial Operating System.

One of the first exercises in his book *Traction* is about creating workplace values. Creating workplace values is not the same as setting individual values, which we did on page 18. Creating workplace values is about defining the heart of a business and identifying the values that are critical to a company's success. After all, your personal values are just that. And while you would be unfulfilled if your company flat-out violated your personal values, your business's values are not necessarily the same as your personal values.

Your business values have to allow for your personal values to thrive, of course, but they do not need to be the same. Your company likely has a set of values based on your professional vision. You might, for instance, value adventure on a personal level, but to support your love of extreme sports and travel, you need your company to avoid risk, play it safe, and be consistent.

So how do you find your company's values? Here is an abbreviated explanation of Wickman's process: Think of the employees in your office who are indispensible. If you could clone these employees, your company would take over the world. Once you have identified a handful of these people, write down the value characteristics that they display in their work.

You might come up with things like:

- Unequivocal excellence
- Committed to quality
- Wins
- Does the right thing
- Compassionate
- Honest
- Integrity
- Hungry for achievement
- Enthusiastic
- Energetic
- Tenacious
- Competitive
- Encourages individual creativity
- Encourages individual ability
- Accountable
- Customer above all else
- Hard worker
- Never satisfied
- Helps first
- Exhibits professionalism
- Exhibits initiative
- Growth-oriented
- Treats all with respect
- Not entitled
- Encourages
- Dreams

- Imagines
- Creative
- Lacks cynicism
- Modest and humble
- Confident
- Consistent

- Committed
- Pays attention to reputation
- Fun
- Fair
- Team player
- Dependable

- Ethical
- Decisive
- Goal-oriented
- Grateful
- Orderly

Some of these values will be position-specific. For instance, a person who works with customers might demonstrate the value of helping others first, whereas the bookkeeper might be extremely honest and ethical. These values are important, but more informative in this context are the shared values. What are the values that your top performers share across the board?

If your top performers—the ones you want to clone—all exhibit these values, stop hiring people unless they too share these values! This is how your team can become aligned with your business's values. If, for instance, all of your peak performers are consistently dependable, committed to quality, and growth-oriented team players who are effective and efficient, start hiring people who share this profile. These values will naturally start emerging as part of your brand, which will pay off in dividends when it comes to having lasting relationships with your clients.

Allocating Responsibilities Through the Human Capital Organizational Chart

Your team will be much stronger if each individual person is working within his or her value set, intelligences, and conation. A great way to make sure that employees are tasked with the right duties is through the human capital organizational chart.

You likely have an organizational chart that depicts each role on your team, as well as the responsibilities associated with each role. How about starting a different organization chart that lists the intelligences, values, and striving instincts (conations) that are specific to each role within the organization?

The bookkeeper's role might look like this:

- Intelligences: math/scientific
- Values: hard work, honesty, frugality, precision
- Striving instinct: fact finder, follow through

The person who acts as the front line when answering phones might look like this:

- Intelligences: interpersonal
- Values: community, harmony, service
- Striving instinct: follow through, accommodating quick start

Do this for every position on your team, and then get to know your employees. You can do this through several tools:

1. To learn more about the different types of intelligences a person might exhibit, read Howard Gardner's *Multiple Intelligences.*
2. For more about your team members' values, ask your employees to complete the values exercise on page 18.
3. Administer a Kolbe A and Kolbe B on your team members to learn more about their natural striving modes. Kolbe also has a tool called RightFit™, which assists in analyzing potential hires. Or, better yet, find a certified Kolbe consultant in your area by visiting www.kolbe.com.

This might seem like a massive amount of work, so you certainly do not need to conquer this with each team member immediately. Start with the departments or employees who are not being as efficient or productive as you would like and consider that there might be a gap between the intelligences, values, and conations you need them to exhibit per your human capital organizational chart, and the intelligences, values, and conations that they naturally exhibit.

CHAPTER 2

Social Capital

Relationships matter.

Consider Lululemon Athletica Inc.

A relative newcomer to the athletic apparent industry, Lululemon is a success story by any measure, despite its fair share of negative publicity. It opened its first store in Vancouver in 2000. In 2003, it opened its first U.S.-based store. By the first quarter of 2013, Lululemon operated 211 stores, primarily in North America. The company's revenue increased from $40.7 million in its 2004 fiscal year to $1.370 billion in its 2012–2013 fiscal year. This translates into an enviable 55 percent compound annual growth rate. Did I mention this was for luxury sportswear, and during a recession?

Perhaps more impressive than a luxury sportswear business thriving during a recession is that the growth didn't come from new stores only. Same-store sales increased 16 percent in 2012–2013, during which time Lululemon stores ranked among the top North American retail stores in sales-per-square-foot at $2,058.

Through solid intellectual capital, Lululemon admittedly developed a fantastic product: high-performance women's sportswear. Filling a void in the marketplace, its apparel combines performance, fit, and comfort with style. Whereas an old T-shirt and a pair of baggy shorts used to be sufficient workout gear, Lululemon has created a culture of fashion-conscious gym-goers. Of course, the workout gear is functional as well: It has technical fabrics that wick moisture away, invisible seams for comfort, and flattering cuts.

And it truly has become a brand associated with luxury. A friend of mine told me that she received an invitation to a fundraiser for her child's exclusive private school with these instructions: *Come comfortable. Wear your lulus.*

Lulu's product itself, though, is not patented. When Lululemon releases a new piece of sportswear, large competitors quickly develop similar products.

What sets Lululemon apart is its social capital. Indeed, it is difficult to think of a company that has made better use of social capital than Lululemon. According to its Form 10-K annual growth report, Lululemon is marketed through "influential fitness practitioners who embrace and create excitement around [its] brand" (Lululemon Athletica Corporation). In other words, Lululemon recognizes that fitness instructors have a strong degree of influence within their communities, so the company builds social capital with this group.

Lululemon identifies popular Pilates, yoga, boot camp, and running instructors who have large networks and strong reputations in communities where Lululemon has a retail presence. These instructors are then invited to choose a free outfit at the nearest Lululemon retail location. In exchange for a 15 percent ongoing discount on all Lululemon merchandise, instructors are asked to become part of Lululemon's research and development team, which means these instructors are required to give product feedback three times a year.

The feedback requirement gives Lululemon valuable information about its products, but more importantly, it enables the company to develop an ongoing relationship with the local fitness instructors.

The strategy works. Since its inception, Lululemon sportswear has sprouted and then multiplied in gyms and fitness studios across North America. The once-unknown brand is popular among instructors and their students, but the company's social capital continues to be a driving focus.

In fact, Lululemon developed relationships with instructors even more fully through its Ambassador program. Ambassadors are elite instructors chosen by Lululemon to work with a specific store. Instructors apply for the opportunity to be a Lululemon ambassador and are chosen based on commitment to their community, their sport, and the Lululemon lifestyle. Instructors who are chosen to be ambassadors are honored by Lululemon employees, who often deliver the news at the ambassador's home gym with signs, cupcakes, or some other form of fanfare. The congratulatory party is an event for the ambassador, as well as all the students who are at the gym. It marks the beginning of a relationship.

Ambassadors' only financial compensation is $1,000 of free apparel, which they model in their own classes and in their Lululemon store. In return, ambassadors host in-store events such as yoga classes and run clubs. They work closely with Lululemon employees to generate excitement about the brand. One ambassador wrote that she feels part of the Lululemon family.

This is social capital at work: After all, influential instructors became totally invested in the Lululemon store's success.

And so do customers. Remember when I said that the ambassadors held in-store yoga classes and run clubs? These events are free and open to the public, giving the store a strong presence within a community.

This isn't the only way Lululemon builds social capital with its customers. Store employees write customers' names on white boards located on dressing room doors, and because the store has strategically placed folding tables in the center room that houses individual dressing room stalls, employees can chat with customers while they try on clothes. Store employees call the customers by names, ask them questions about their fitness needs, showing interest in their lives and goals, thereby building rapport and loyal customers.

I would be remiss if I failed to mention that Lululemon's strong social capital was built upon a rich human capital. The company has consistently communicated a set of values that resonate with employees, customers, and instructors. One of its goals, for instance, is to elevate the world from mediocrity to greatness. With this value in mind, it is no wonder the store's employees are able to maintain a high level of optimism and a friendly demeanor when interacting with customers, whom the store refers to as guests.

Now consider what happened when Lululemon's founder breached that relationship by seemingly blaming the company's too-sheer yoga pants on women who have large thighs. Women of all shapes and sizes came forward to accuse the company of fat bashing (their term, not mine!). Social media lit up with people vowing to boycott the store. In the end, the founder resigned because he damaged the social capital too much to continue acting as head of the company. He and the company knew that social capital matters far too much to keep the company's founder at the helm.

On a personal level, we already know that relationships matter. We (hopefully) honor our most important relationships. But Lululemon demonstrates something that is less-often considered: Just as an individual's life becomes more valuable if it is enriched through social connections, so too will a business become more valuable if it is rich in social capital.

Whom does your organization serve? Who serves your organization? And, who are the people that you, your partners, and your employees know? This defines your social capital, which is further gauged by the strength of these relationships and the extent to which they can be accessed as a resource for your organization.

Think back to my friend (and client) John, whose bank was about to close on him, but who was able to pull himself out of his hole due to his strong relationships. John found a way out of this mess for one reason and one reason only: He had a lot of strong relationships that he had nurtured throughout the years. He understood something that many people overlook: The relationships you have with the different types of people in your life all constitute a form of capital that can be leveraged in the future. You get something from the relationship—some form of money that you can spend.

To be clear, my intention is not to recommend promoting social capital by manipulation. My client who was saved by his social capital did not purpose to enhance his social capital for social capital's sake. He did this because it affirmed his values. One of his several intelligences was interpersonal, and he naturally used that characteristic.

If maintaining social relationships does not come naturally, what can you do to strengthen this capital without becoming manipulative and inauthentic? For one, build a structure so that you are reminded to pay attention to how other decisions will impact your social capital. For instance, when considering bottom-line decisions, ask yourself how this will impact your employees. You can also rely on other people within your network who have stronger interpersonal intelligences than you. Ask a partner or trusted advisor to keep a finger on the pulse of your network so that you do not cause dents in your social capital bank account.

This network includes five groups of people. If you step back and consider all of the people you know, chances are, you can separate all of your relationships into five categories of people with whom you have at least intermittent contact, either personally or professionally:

1. Family members
2. Friends
3. Clients
4. Vendors or service provides (including employees)
5. Business associates

From your family members, you get love. From your friends, you get fun. From clients, you have affiliation, productivity, satisfaction, and accomplishment. Your vendors provide you with a resource—they enable you to deliver your value. And your business associates not only support you but also give you more connections so that you can build more relationships.

These people or groups . . .	Provide you with . . .	Unless you neglect them, in which case you will . . .
Family	Love	Become estranged
Friends	Fun	Miss out on fun and intimacy
Clients	Affiliation, productivity, satisfaction, and accomplishment	Become unproductive
Vendors	Resources	Have fewer available resources and poor methods of delivery
Business associates	Support and connections	Lose business

If you fail to pay attention to these relationships, you can create a negative effect. When you don't foster the relationships with your clients, you will feel less productive, less satisfied, and you will eventually lose business. When you fail to honor your vendors (including employees), your resources will be less available and you will have poor modes of delivery. If you do not treat your friends well, you lose out on a lot of fun and intimacy. And when family members fail to maintain deep roots, they end up estranged.

Just like on a dice, where the opposite of a six is always a one, if you do not intentionally build positive relationships, the opposite will happen: You will erode the relationships.

Obviously, the people who like you will be more likely to help you than the people who do not like you. The reverse is also true: Studies show that dissatisfied customers will tell three or four times more people about their negative experience than satisfied customers will tell about their positive experience. Even if they do not go out of their way to hurt you, the people who dislike you certainly will not provide you with any extra resources.

Consider the person you meet who keeps looking at his smartphone while you exchange pleasantries. This person might have financial capital, but not many people are truly pulling for him. When push comes to shove, he will not have people helping him along the way.

If you want to strengthen your business, paying attention to the people who help you the most, or the people who have the potential to help you the most, allows you to become sticky, meaning these clients, vendors, service providers, employees, and business associates will stick around, even when times are tough.

It bears noting that focusing on social capital, and then intentionally building it to become sticky, can feel disingenuous. No honorable person wants to create relationships that are based on manipulation or deliberate attempts to benefit. So when I encourage people to build social capital with *intention*, I want to point out that I believe true social capital is built on extraordinary degrees of authenticity.

Manipulation Versus Manifestation

If we all agree that social capital is denominated on relationships, we still have an unanswered question: What creates relationships? Healthy, mutually beneficial relationships are based on an understanding of values. You most likely want to associate with people who:

1. Complement you in that their perspectives, skills, or philosophical approaches are different than yours, but somehow make you a better person. In personal relationships, this might manifest as an unlikely

couple. While one spouse might be highly social, the other might be reclusive. The highly social spouse is kept grounded by the recluse; the recluse is kept from retreating into his or her shell. Both spouses benefit.

This might also manifest as a couple with different skill sets. The wife is great at managing money and running a household, but prefers not to have a 9–5 career; the husband is a spendthrift who loves the professional world. Together, they balance each other out.

In business, this relationship is more easily spotted. An employee gives an employer expertise; in turn, the employer gives the employee money. A vendor provides products; in turn, a client delivers money. One business partner specializes in sales and marketing; the other is a long-term visionary who loves imagining and creating new products.

2. Share your values. You and your significant other probably share the same values when it comes to the big things, like raising children. You and your best friend might both love to spend the weekends hiking and golfing. And in business, you will likely be drawn to vendors, employees, and clients if you can find common ground. If you are an avid golfer, you might be willing to pay a few extra dollars to a vendor who shows up happy, friendly, and ready to chat a bit about your shared love of the game. And this vendor might have your back if you ever need to request a favor, even because of a small connection, such as a shared love of golf.

One way or another, what binds you to another person is the values that define that relationship, whether they are complementary or commonalities. For the relationship to have longevity, the values that are expressed must be a genuine set of values. We can all sense when someone is being manipulative. This is why I say that rich social capital is build on an extraordinary degree of authenticity.

Many people create these connections without being in conscious touch with their values. They might be able to form relationships with vendors, employees, clients, and business associates, but without a conscious connection to their values, many are unable to form truly sticky relationships. Cultivating relationships can become powerful with that old word: intention.

By this, I mean that there is a difference between saying, "I like him" and saying, "I am committed to him." The only way for a person to feel your commitment is through your words and actions, so the authenticity you feel takes effort and time to express. Being friends with someone on Facebook or connected via LinkedIn does not make a relationship sticky. This only happens when you honor your commitments, intentionally building a relationship, and making sure that a person knows your intention due to the words you say and the actions you take.

Using Social Capital to Become Sticky

We never know a person's or a business's true intention. We can only infer this from the optics. When a person's behavior is being interpreted by the recipient as it was intended, the relationship is authentic. When the person's behavior is being interpreted in a different manner, the relationship is inauthentic. Relationships built on complementary or common values become sticky when a person is able to infer another person's intention with a high degree of accuracy.

If a company, for instance, claims to value its customers, but its customers have a hard time reaching an actual human being when they call a support line, the customers will feel disconnected from the company's stated intention. They will infer that the company does not care about its customers.

This is exactly what happened to Netflix back in 2011. Netflix was founded in 1997 by Marc Randolph and the now-CEO Reed Hastings. At the time, Netflix revolutionized the movie rental business with its innovative structure. Subscribers could log into an easy-to-use website and order DVDs for delivery directly to their front door. After paying who-knows-how-much-money in late fees to the big-wig video rental stores, now customers could keep DVDs as long as they liked without incurring late fees. Making it even more convenient, once they returned a DVD, the next selection in their personal queue was shipped out.

Netflix went on to build a streaming platform that was compatible with hundreds of devices, enabling subscribers to download movies instantaneously.

In early 2011, Netflix was enjoying tremendous success. Shares of the company increased 200 percent in 2010, and Reed Hastings was widely recognized as a visionary leader.

And so Hastings embarked on a plan to keep Netflix on the cutting edge. It was clear to Hastings that streaming, and not DVD rentals, was the future of the business. Yet acquiring content for streaming was more difficult and more expensive than Hastings had anticipated, so in July 2011, Hastings announced a price increase that would be effective in September. Instead of a $10 monthly fee for both streaming and DVD services, customers would be charged $7.99 a month for streaming and $7.99 a month for DVD services—or $15.98 for both services.

It was a cost difference of $6 a month, which represented an effective 60 percent price increase for those choosing to retain both services. Customers were outraged. Granted the price increase was just $6, but it was steep in percentage terms. Say what you want about whether the outrage was justified: Netflix certainly did not think so.

Days after the price increase was announced, Netflix's spokesperson responded to customers' negative reaction by saying that this $6 increase is still "a remarkable value, a latte or two every month. For most folks it's absorbable" (Chansanchai 2011).

In effect, Netflix responded by disregarding their customers' concerns. Hastings himself brushed off the criticism, claiming that the company wouldn't lose many subscribers.

By October 2011, Netflix had lost 600,000 subscribers and the company stock had nosedived from over $300 a share to under $80 a share.

It bears noting that most analysts agreed that a price increase was necessary, and that Netflix's emphasis on the streaming business made perfect strategic sense. In fact, the strategy was proven successful in the long term; it was a difficult uphill battle, but by early 2014 Netflix was trading at $400 a share.

In the short term, though, something went terribly wrong. Hastings blurred lines and totally overestimated Netflix's relationship with its customers. His announcements and decisions demonstrated a basic lack of understanding of what his customers did and did not care about. To many people who are pinching pennies and weathering a recession, $6 a month *is* a lot of money, especially when it is piled on top of other expenses. And when a corporation and its wealthy CEOs fail to realize this, its customers will retaliate.

Subscribers were unhappy with the price increase, but the outrage likely had more to do with its poor communication. Instead of acknowledging that this was a significant price increase, Netflix minimized the concerns of its customers.

Clients, employees, vendors, and business associates all have one central question when it comes to their relationships with you: *Does this person care for me?* If the answer is *yes*, they want your intention to be obvious. If Netflix cares about its customers (and I believe that it does), the customers want to feel like they matter. If that appreciation is ambiguous, the rest can come crashing down. If a certified public accountant gives tax advice to someone, and that person infers that the advice is a guise for the CPA's hidden desire to increase her billable hours, the client interprets the CPA's intention as disingenuous. The advisor's behavior is interpreted as being self-oriented rather than client-oriented.[1]

On the other hand, if a patient infers that a doctor is highly compassionate, the patient will likely be less likely to sue for bad outcomes than if the patient believes the doctor is cold and uncaring.

As a business owner, pay attention to the optics of how you deliver your product or service. Pay attention to how you deal with vendors and employees. And pay attention to how your associates infer your intentions.

There's an old wives' tale (though some swear it is true) that Nordstrom once refunded a customer for a tire—even though Nordstrom has never sold tires.

The company has intentionally created a brand of having a no-hassle return policy. Customers can return an item without its tags and without its receipt. Nordstrom does this because it understands optics. It wants its customers to *see* that Nordstrom truly believes that the customer is always right. Nordstrom knows that it will have a stronger reputation and richer social capital if its customers infer its intentions.

Did a Nordstrom employee really give someone a refund on a tire, even though the tire clearly wasn't purchased at the clothing store? We can never know for sure, but if this is an old wives' tale, then it is an even stronger indication of the optics surrounding Nordstrom. The company has built such strong consumer relations that legends have been told!

When your business has successful transactions, as Nordstrom obviously has, your social capital account gets richer. Your well of relationships begins to fill. Every time you add another successful transaction, you get more and more credit.

The problem is that negative inferences created by lapses of structure (and therefore values that are not honored) will always deplete the account. And these negative transactions will deplete the account with a greater magnitude than the credit you would enjoy under a successful transaction. It might be unfair, but the truth is that it takes a lifetime to build a reputation and a minute to kill it.

I was recently in Nevada with a client who was considering hiring a new lawyer. Together, we went to a conference to meet with one of the firms in the running to represent this wealthy client of mine. Instead of taking us to one of the well-appointed conference rooms, the attorney led us through the working floors to an office in the back. I can only assume why the law firm would make this tactical mistake. Perhaps they thought my client, who values hardworking people, wanted to see the inner workings of the law firm.

Regardless, the working rooms of a law firm are a disaster—kind of like the working rooms of a CPA firm. Every office was tiny and jam-packed with files, and almost every single office looked like it had been invaded by Gremlins. Optically, the firm looked messy. Immediately after we left the meeting, my client mentioned that if the firm's offices were that messy, its work might be sloppy as well. The attorney lost the opportunity to impress my client even before we entered the workroom to hold the meeting.

If your social capital is already strong, then you might be given a pass on one or two negative transactions. But if you have too many, you will wipe out the entire relationship. On the other hand, if you build an account of strong social capital, you can stave off many threats.

Here are three ideas for building and protecting your social capital potential. Consider making shifts in the following:

1. The way you treat casual relationships.
2. The degree of intimacy you infer, and whether you are blurring the lines.
3. Your social capital.

The Power of Casual Relationships

One way you can protect your social capital is by focusing your attention on the effects of your behavior through the power of casual relationships. Imagine that you take all the people in your life and place them around you in concentric circles based on your degree of intimacy. It might look something like the following diagram.

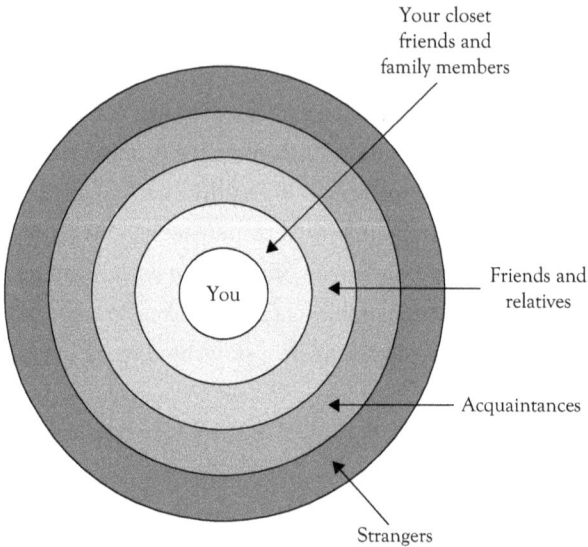

The inner circle represents you. Directly around you are all of your closest friends, spouse, and immediate family members. Then come your good friends. Next are acquaintances, and finally strangers, who are people you do not know, but might know of, like your grandfather's ex-stepdaughter from his second wife, or your best friend's old college roommate.

Taking a look at the concentric circles, which relationships do you think are the most important in terms of helping you or your business grow?

Most people would say that friends and family members are the most important. And certainly, your closest friends and family members are the people who are most important to you and your quality of life. But I argue that in terms of forming new business opportunities, the more distant a relationship is, the more powerful it can be.

This seems counterintuitive, but think of it like Facebook. You and your closest friend probably have a ton of mutual friends. You know everyone that your best friend knows. So while your relationship with this friend is near and dear to your heart, it holds less promise of generating new relationships that you can incorporate into your life. After all, you already know most of the same people.

Now think about someone you don't know very well. You and this person have very few (if any) mutual friends. This person, therefore, could be a powerhouse in terms of his or her ability to introduce you to new people who can help you build your business, or otherwise enrich your life. Those people can connect you to more people and sets of people.

If you are the sun, the planets farthest away from you will be the most meaningful when creating new, exciting, and surprising opportunities.

I call this "The Power of Casual Relationships."

One of my friends, Mike, is a well-connected lobbyist. When it came time for my son, then a law-school student, to get an internship, I asked Mike whom he knew who might be able to write a letter recommending my son for an internship in the district attorney's office.

Mike said, "Gary! Gary could do it."

Gary is Mike's long-term friend. Gary, in turn, is an old friend of the district attorney. Up until that time, Gary and I had not spent enough time together to be anything other than acquaintances, but because both of us are good friends with Mike, and because we are generally good guys, I knew Gary would help my son out by writing a letter to the district attorney on my behalf.

My son ended up getting the internship. Did Gary's intervention help? Well, it certainly did not hurt.

Often, we fail to spend time with distant relationships or create new relationships with strangers. We think: *Why waste time on people I barely know when I know so many people whose company I already know I enjoy?* The power of casual relationships explains why it is important to nurture these relationships. The most opportunity lies in stepping foot in new and distant territories. When you keep to your own group, you will be less likely to hear new ideas and expand your own perception of what is possible. You will become insulated, unaware of the different people out there who are doing new and innovative things. Meeting new people allows you to become stimulated with new ideas and outlooks.

This is not to say that you should ignore your closest friends. On a personal level, these friendships *are* the most important. I am probably not going to think about my casual acquaintances while I am on my deathbed, and I am definitely not going to think about strangers when I reflect back on my best memories of life. From a professional point of view, though, my casual acquaintances and I have more opportunities for strengthening our social capital than we do with our closest friends and family members.

Indeed, Gary and I have become much closer now that we've nurtured our once-casual friendship. I like him, and he likes me. Gary recently contacted me to ask if I could connect him with some people who could assist him with a business problem he had. This connection from Mike has made all of our social capital networks richer. Now that I have become friends with Gary, I have a whole new layer of casual relationships to nurture!

The Capitals and Me

Consider all of the people you know in each of the five areas. Then name five acquaintances or strangers in each category. These are people you do not know well or at all but provide promise for growth and opportunities in your profession:

1. Who are the distant family members who might make great contacts for you?
2. Who are the acquaintances that you could get to know better? We all have friends that we haven't gotten to know as well as we could.
3. What about clients? Do you have clients who could introduce you to other people?
4. And who are the vendors or service providers who might be able to introduce you to other people?
5. Finally, which business associates are great targets?

Remember, in personal life, the same elements hold true. Social relationships can serve you in the same way professional relationships can serve you. If you are always warm and friendly to your handyman, he will be happy to help you find a reputable plumber when a pipe breaks.

Living in a State of Lack

As you begin to build your social capital with intention, pay attention to the effect your closest friends and family members have on you. Dan Sullivan of the Strategic Coach has an interesting perspective when it comes to building relationships. Dan asks all of his students to target five people who have a bigger future. These, he told me, are people "whose batteries are included."

If you surround yourself with people who are sucking energy from you as opposed to running on their own power, you will start living in a state of lack. You will not have enough energy to feed yourself.

I won't ask you to write this down, but take a moment to consider the people in your life with whom you spend the most time. Are their batteries included? If so, your energy will feed off theirs, and together, you will give each other energy in the forms of encouragement, support, or healthy competition.

You know when a friend or family member is sucking the life out of you. Acknowledge it, even if it is only in your mind. You might not be able to distance yourself entirely from these people, but be sure to have enough batteries-included people close to you who can counter the ill-effects of those people who are sucking energy from you.

Blurred Lines

Undoubtedly, each of the five main classifications of relationships—family members, friends, clients, vendors or service providers, and business associations—has different characteristics. Trouble starts to brew, though, when lines become blurry.

The Friend Zone

Friends and family members, for instance, can become clients, vendors, or business associates. This relationship comes with its own set of problems.

When my firm provides accountancy or legacy planning services for a friend or family member, I am reticent to bill. When we hired my niece, I worried whether this nepotism would cause problems with her coworkers. And what would it do to my relationship with her—and with my sister (her mother)—if she didn't pull her own weight?

The lines became blurred because my intentions were blurred. With respect to my niece, I have two possibly contradictory intentions: First, I want her to know how loved and valued she is as my niece. In fact, in this regard, my love is unconditional. On the other hand, if she is to remain my employee, she must meet certain conditions that are required of anyone in this position.

I had to be careful so that she inferred both of these from my intentions. In an effort to make sure she inferred my unconditional personal love, I might have failed to communicate my high expectations for her as an employee. If she then dropped the ball, I might have been forced to fire her, which would have come as a shock given that she inferred my intentions as 100 percent unconditional.

Fortunately, both my niece and I were able to communicate our intentions, so these concerns were avoided. I created a virtual wall between my relationship with her and my relationship with her job. Her supervisors have absolute authority to handle her as they would any other employee, and I have never intervened in any matter related to her employment at my firm. Her employment has been successful, but we all know the inherent dangers of crossing the line from personal to professional.

On the flip side are the relationships that seemingly transition from professional to personal, an evolution that has a different texture. It is with these relationships that I am more concerned. One surefire way to jeopardize the strength of a relationship is to infer a degree of intimacy inappropriate for a relationship. As relationships change and grow, entrepreneurs often miscalculate the intimacy of a relationship and begin treating a relationship that is first and foremost a business relationship as a friendship instead.

Many years ago, this happened in our office. For a decade, we had a large client who paid our firm in the neighborhood of $40,000 each year. One of our partners grew close with the client. My partner and this client invited each other for holiday parties and family gatherings. Their families took trips together. Our client even asked my business partner to be in his wedding.

Then one year, our client asked us to provide additional services above and beyond what we normally did for him. As a result, his bill was larger than usual. The client became furious. He called my partner in shock: *How dare we charge extra money! Wasn't our firm willing to do a simple favor? Aren't they friends, after all?*

The reality is this: While my business partner might have considered the friendship to be more important than the professional relationship, our firm considered him to be a client, first and foremost. And because the client and my partner blurred the lines between personal and professional, we lost a client, and my partner lost a friend.

Our client (and my partner's friend) failed to understand that the relationship was one with the firm and not just with the partner. Friends give friends favors, but companies that constantly give favors soon go out of business.

The lesson? Be aware of who you are with and the circumstances of a relationship. Although you might socialize with a client, or even consider a client to be a close friend, remember that as long as you are doing business together, the business relationship will probably trump the personal relationship. And if it doesn't—if your friendship truly has grown so that the personal relationship outweighs the importance of the business relationship—consider ending the business relationship.

One way or another, pay attention to the optics.

No matter how much I like a client, I will never drink much alcohol in front of the client, even if this is someone I have known a very long time. (Fortunately, I am not someone who likes to drink a lot of alcohol anyway, so this is an easy standard to keep.) The big concern here is this: Why would any client ever want to deal with an accountant who is ever out of control?

I have known business relationships that end, all because one person inferred a degree of intimacy and, therefore, behaved inappropriately in front of someone who was primarily a professional contact.

I attended a conference in Las Vegas one year, and on the second day of the conference, I heard rumors that a huge firm (and one of my competitors) had lost an important client that very day.

Why?

On the previous night, one of the firm's accountants ran into a client who was on vacation in Las Vegas. Both the accountant and the client were seated at a blackjack table, where they remained seated all night. According to the story, they had a great time together, but the client decided that the accountant was not someone he wanted touching his money.

When he returned to his hotel room in the wee hours of the morning, he called the firm's front office and left a message terminating their relationship.

It was a great opportunity for Rose, Snyder, and Jacobs to solicit a new client, and it was a lesson for every single accountant at the conference: Maintain a high degree of professional integrity in front of your clients, even while cutting loose and having fun.

Your actions in a professional and social setting will be evidence that another person will use to infer competence and character. The accountant found sitting at the blackjack table should have promptly said good night and told the client that he was returning to his room. The night might not have been as much fun, but the client would have interpreted his behavior as significantly more responsible.

So be aware that nurturing a relationship does not mean that you start treating everyone like your best friend. Honor what the relationship is, and then strengthen it within those boundaries.

For instance, when you ask a vendor for a favor, remember that no matter how much you like the vendor, and vice versa, he or she is not going to provide you with a no-strings-attached favor. Only your intimate friends and family members care enough about your self-interest to truly provide a favor void of their own self-interest. Vendors will always attach a price tag in a quid-pro-quo fashion. They might not expect you to pay now, but they will expect you to pay in some way at some point in the future.

If you acknowledge and honor this, you will be less likely to cross boundaries that jeopardize this relationship. That is not to say that a business would never take advantage of its social capital bank account. Just know that the funds are limited.

Employees Are . . . Vendors?

Although most businesses would place employees in the category of business associates, I argue that they are more closely aligned with the category of vendors for one reason: Employees usually do not share your risk, at least not to a large degree.

This is where business owners often get into trouble when it comes to acknowledging and nurturing their relationship with employees. Whereas a business associate will have interests that you both share, an employee has his or her own self-interest. The relationship between the employer and employee is usually symbiotic. Just as you have a selfish interest when hiring an employee (you want to increase your company's productivity and, therefore, its profitability), your employees have their own selfish interest, usually in the form of cold, hard, cash.

At its very core, the employer–employee relationship is a business deal. The employee agrees to do X, Y, and Z, and the employer agrees to pay the employee in return.

Yes, they want you and your business to succeed. If the relationship is a healthy one, the employee is a cheerleader for you and your organization. To be certain, they are closer and more invested in your company than the office-supply vendor down the street.

Yet your employees' investment into your company is ultimately only as deep as their paycheck. If you stop paying your employees, they will not stick around for long. I'm not being cynical here. This is the way it *ought* to be. Most employees are at work first and foremost to support themselves and their families—not to protect your dream.

Often, though, employers are surprised and discouraged when employees exhibit their own self-interest, sometimes at the expense of a business. But truly, shouldn't employees look out for themselves and try to protect their time, families, resources, and personal fulfillment? Isn't this what you did when you started climbing the corporate ladder or when you started your business?

We all have self-interests. This is only logical, and when we start honoring our employees as vendors and inferring their behavior accordingly, we can begin improving our relationships with them. If we ask them to work weekends or extended shifts, we must remember that we are asking a vendor to perform a favor. Just as you would be reticent to ask your paper supplier to wash the dishes, be reticent to ask your employees to perform duties outside of the agreement you originally negotiated with them, especially if you are not going to offer increased compensation.

These favors have a price tag, and if you do not repay the favor later down the road, the employees will become bitter—all because the employer did not acknowledge the characteristics of the relationship.

Just as an employee should not believe that he or she has a right to a position, an owner should not believe that he or she has a right to demand increased time or production from the employee. The employee–employer relationship gets twisted when employers use their position to exploit their employees.

Think of it like this: Imagine that you hired a college student to babysit your children at a rate of $10, and she agrees to work every Friday night. On Saturday, you need someone to help you move into a new home, so you call your babysitter and demand that she come and help you carry heavy boxes into the moving truck in 97-degree weather. Does this seem fair?

While it would be appropriate to *ask* the babysitter to help, and to then *negotiate* pay, it would not be appropriate to demand performance.

The key here is an open communication process. Employees can make or break your company, so have the uncomfortable conversations, even when it is easier to sweep them under a rug. This means that you do the following:

- Be specific about what their duties are.
- Ask them—and ask them often—what you can do to improve.
- When you sense tension, invite your employee to lunch and talk about the problem. If you intentionally build a culture that allows open communication, and if you understand that the employee–employer relationship is a business agreement, this needn't be hostile.
- Tell your employees when they are not meeting your expectations. If you do not communicate this to your employees immediately, they will be confused when you fire them, and they will be much more likely to file a lawsuit against you.

I have a friend who hired a nanny for her children. The nanny arrives to work 10 minutes late every day. My friend is irritated because this means that she starts her day frantic. She regularly complains about this problem. Of course, it seems obvious that her employee should report to work on time, but my friend has never expressed her dissatisfaction directly with her children's nanny. Her dissatisfaction has built and built, and now she is considering firing the nanny—the nanny that has been with her family since her oldest child was four months old.

Wouldn't it be easier to just create an environment where communication is the norm?

Most of all, remember that employees are a resource. If you want to maximize the resources that you get from your vendors or employees, respect and honor these relationships.

Keep in mind, too, the role of shared values. Because an employer and employee usually have competing interests (the employer wants the employee to exhibit less self-interest than the employee will naturally exhibit), some natural friction exists in this relationship. Therefore, the role of shared values becomes critical. If you hire a superstar with the right intelligences and the right instincts, but with values that conflict with yours, the natural antagonism will become pronounced. On the other hand, if you hire someone with shared values, the antagonism will likely be lessened. When interviewing potential employees, look for cues that their values (as described on pages 32–33) will merge nicely with yours.

That said, do not hire a bunch of clones. It is nice to have balance in an office, and remember that different values, intelligences, and conations will fill different roles. But if your top values are solitude and productivity, you might want to think twice about hiring the class clown as your assistant, even if he displays the right intelligences and right instincts for the job.

Great Customers, Raving Fans

Every company has at least one: A paying client who is also a pain in the proverbial. Hopefully, every company also has at least one raving fan—a customer who adores the company and all of its team members and is therefore a piece of cake.

What are the attributes that make the model customer so desirable? Why is the first client such a pain in the you-know-what?

Every company should be able to answer these questions. You will have a far easier time targeting ideal customers if you can create an avatar that represents the qualities shared by your best customers, and another avatar that represents the qualities shared by your worst customers.

If you can pack your social network with clients who are raving fans, and limit your exposure to those who are difficult, you will benefit from great referrals. (And as a side note, you will also spend less time holding your clients' hands and managing complaints and more time building your capitals.)

Social Capital and Social Media

One of my vendors is a rock star in terms of his abilities. He is reliable, knowledgeable, and incredibly dedicated. He has served our firm for years, and he recently came to me asking for a fulltime position. Our human resources director, who is ultimately in charge of hiring him, was skeptical. Among other things, the vendor had failed to separate his personal life from his professional life on his social media sites. When he makes a political rant, we all see it—and half of us do not agree with his politics. When he gets drunk at a bar on the weekend, he posts pictures. He sure looks like he is having fun, but he sure does not look like someone we want to represent of our firm.

It just doesn't look good optically.

I am not the first person to point out the dangers of comingling a personal life and a professional life on social media, and I certainly will not be the last. It bears mentioning, though, because it is important. What do your clients, employees, vendors, and associates infer about your social media sites? And do these inferences line up with what you intend to have happened for your business?

If social media is used in a way that honors a company's intentions, it can strengthen the social capital of an organization. Now, I want to give a slightly unorthodox example here, in part because I think it makes for easy and fun reading. So please excuse my deviation out of the corporate world into the world of entertainment.

In the summer of 2013, the Syfy Channel aired *Sharknado*, a ridiculously improbable made-for-television movie about a tornado that lifted sharks out of the ocean and dropped them into swimming pools, the flooded streets, and water spouts all around Los Angeles. The movie was, by all accounts, terrible. The dialog was campy, the acting was mediocre at best, and the story line was obnoxious and unbelievable.

It should come as no surprise, then, that when it premiered, *Sharknado* didn't do as well as most Syfy original firms, garnering 1.37 million viewers, a little less than the average audience of 1.5 million viewers.

But here's the astonishing part: *Sharknado* aired again a week later to an audience of 1.89 million viewers. And about 10 days later, a third airing garnered 2.1 million viewers. This was a Syfy record—*Sharknado* was the most watched original film encore in Syfy's history.

All of this was thanks to Twitter, on which #Sharknado was definitely trending.

Syfy knows how to use social media to build its social capital. During the original airing of *Sharknado*, the channel aired tweets from viewers on the bottom of the screen. This only encouraged people to head to Twitter to post their catchy and/or snarky *Sharknado* jokes.

Actor, comedian, director, and screenwriter B. J. Novak tweeted: "I'm afraid that now when we have a real sharknado everyone's going to treat it like a joke."

Christina Applegate tweeted a line from the movie: "We can't just stay here and let sharks rain down on us . . ."

Even the Red Cross had something to say about *Sharknado*. "We're ready to respond if there is a #Sharknado," tweeted the Red Cross Oklahoma. "If it were to happen, it would be in Oklahoma. Why? Because we're tough like that."

Craig Engler, senior vice president at Syfy Digital, runs the @Syfy Twitter handle. "We know going in that people already love to tweet about these movies, so our goal is to foster the conversation and amplify it. For instance, we'll retweet fun posts from our viewers on the @Syfy feed, which the fans love. It gives them their 15 minutes of fame on Twitter and shows them that we're listening and playing along."

And all this Twitter fame encourages those not watching to tune in next time.

American Idol, the *X Factor*, and *America's Got Talent* all leverage social capital to create a shared experience for millions of viewers while using

Twitter to create a stronger connection with their viewers. This is social media at its best!

So what can you do to focus on your social capital? Here are a few pointers:

1. Remember to be intentional. Start by listing the connections you have in each of the five categories. Then ask yourself what you can do to make yourself stickier with the key players in your professional categories. Have you and your company created standards of behavior to let these connections know that they are important to you.

2. When important decisions are being made in your business, be aware of the effect of these decisions on your social capital. What might your customers say, for instance, when their calls are routed through an intricate voice mail system?

3. Make an effort to pay more attention to the distant social capital connections you might make. Ask your closer connections who they might appreciate getting to know in your world. And then ask them if they know anyone you might want to know.

CHAPTER 3

Structural Capital

If intellectual capital is the thought—the copyright, the patent, or the piece of steel—then structural capital is the mechanism by which your company delivers that thought to the end user in the form of a product or a service.

Structural capital is defined by how your company shares its knowledge and communicates with its social capital through a unique process. It includes your organization's systems and processes, as well as its modes and styles of communication. Among many other examples, a company could have a process for the following:

- Transferring knowledge to new employees through an employee handbook.
- Invoicing its clients, and then addressing outstanding invoices in a way that protects its bottom line (financial capital) and still honors its client or customer relationships (social capital).
- Delivering its service.
- Maintaining its social networking sites.
- Creating its product.
- Pitching a product or service to prospective clients.

The Glue That Holds the Capitals Together

To a certain extent, structural capital is the glue that holds all of the other four capitals together. It represents everything that occurs between the thought and the expression of that thought. A company with rich structural capital will have a process (or a set of processes) that makes sure: (1) its human capital is honored through its actions; (2) its social capital is not only being protected but also being leveraged; (3) its intellectual capital is delivered efficiently; and (4) its bottom line is, therefore, maximized.

To a certain extent, then, structural capital is the most important. Yet it also is the most ignored capital. Although other business books and thought leaders have studied the four other capitals, structural capital seems to be lightly considered or reduced to tomes that focus on logistics or processes. I have always sensed that most businesses (and advisors) consider structural capital to be a thing and not an asset. But for a business to truly thrive, structural capital needs to be elevated and honored in the same way a bank account, a customer, or product is.

This oversight is surprising: If a business has human, intellectual, and social capital that can affect the financial capital, but it does not have a good process for bringing all this together, can the company ever get paid?

Absolutely not. The company is just plain leaking money.

It stands to reason, then, that structural capital offers a business the most room for improvement. It is this capital that gives a company richness of dimension. Companies can only sustain themselves if they deliver some kind of value to the end user. That delivery system, whether intentional or not, is the company's structural capital. The stronger the structural capital, the more likely the company will be sustainable.

In fact, I argue that a company could have a shoddy product or offer a substandard service, but have great structures for securing new clients, building rapport, providing customer service, and following up on accounts receivable. Because of this company's strong structural capital, it would likely fare much better than a company with a superior service or product that does not know how to market to its target clients, communicate with them, or collect money from them.

Case in point: Webvan.

Webvan was founded in 1999 in San Francisco during the heyday of online investing. With revenue of only $4 million, Webvan raised $375 million in an initial public offering, and then it went on to raise a total of $800 million from investors. At its peak, Webvan had a valuation of $1.2 billion.

With padded coffers paving its way, Webvan expanded rapidly, traveling from San Francisco to Chicago, to Dallas, DC, Seattle, and Atlanta.

By 2001, just two short years later, Webvan was bankrupt.

So what went wrong? It was not the concept. The concept was innovative. Investors were clearly excited about it, and Webvan's grocery-deliver service met a real need. Other companies, most notably Fresh Direct, have since turned the concept into a profitable business. And the product Webvan offered was not inferior. In 2000, Webvan was voted the best online grocery for three consecutive quarters, indicating that customers were quite satisfied with the product.

A widely cited reason for Webvan's failure was that it expanded too quickly, but this was not it. In fact, later in this chapter, you will learn about a company that based its impressive success on a business model that *required* expedient growth.

No, the problem was not simply quick expansion. The more accurate explanation is that Webvan expanded a business model that was structurally flawed. At the same time it was expanding into other regions, Webvan was failing in its original stores in the San Francisco market.

Webvan invested heavily in facilities and software. It built expensive, high-tech distributions centers at a cost of $30 million a pop. The distribution centers were fully automated and housed miles of conveyor belts, as well as a computer system of lights that showed employees where to pick products. Webvan estimated that this automated system was 10 times more productive than a traditional shopper picking groceries.

The company also developed proprietary software to take orders and manage deliveries. When it came to investing in the best, most efficient software out there, Webvan spared no expense.

All the bells and whistled sizzled, for sure, but its facilities were out of proportion with the size of the business, and not by just a little bit. It built these high fixed costs into an industry with margins under two percent, which required ambitious, unrealistic break-even volume.

But more importantly, Webvan put most of its resources in order fulfillment and neglected to optimize structure in an area that was more critical to the success of the business: route efficiency.

Webvan's most serious mistake was in not limiting its service areas to densely populated regions where travel times between stops were minimal. The company serviced sparsely populated suburban areas that required more fuel, time, and labor for each delivery.

Perhaps, Webvan thought that these more remote areas were most in need of a grocery-delivery service. But were they really? Reflect on all those typecasts of suburban households, with their minivans and soccer moms. Now think about the hustle and bustle of city life, with its single folks, its two-working-parent households, and its never-ending traffic.

With ample parking, less traffic, and smaller crowds, suburban areas offer a more pleasant shopping experience than crowded urban grocery stores.

Webvan compounded the problem by guaranteeing half-hour delivery windows, forcing the company not only to increase manpower, but also to schedule even more inefficient routes.

Now contrast Webvan to Fresh Direct, which today is considered the most successful online grocery delivery service. Fresh Direct started in 2004, just a few years after Webvan went out of business. Fresh Direct is a private company so financial data is not public, but the CEO reported that Fresh Direct has been profitable since 2008 and the company is still growing and expanding into new markets.

Fresh Direct's distribution centers are much less impressive. They are also less expensive. Instead, the company has focused its resources on delivery logistics and website development.

The cherry on top? Fresh Direct targets densely populated areas for delivery. It began in New York City, the most populous city in the United States, and the sixth most-dense city. Specifically, Fresh Direct opened its first store in Manhattan, where it could park a delivery van and make multiple deliveries in one stop. Instead of making half-hour guarantees, the company offers two-hour time slots so it is able to plan efficient delivery routes.

Leveraging the green movement, Fresh Direct's website designates certain timeslots as eco-friendly to indicate that someone in the neighborhood is already getting a delivery during that window, and the company occasionally offers discounts to customers for selecting eco-friendly timeslots. Fresh Direct also developed a detailed customer database and uses it to make targeted shopping suggestions to their customers. The cross marketing tool effectively increases the average dollar amount purchased. Finally, Fresh Direct passes on a small fuel surcharge based on the average retail price of gasoline,

And herein highlights the importance of structural capital: Webvan developed a revolutionary concept, but its delivery structures didn't make sense. Fresh Direct didn't necessarily have a better product, but it had a superior system for delivering the product and a better system to market to target clients. It purposefully developed structural capital that drove profit.

To better understand structural capital, let us take a step back and look at an individual's personal structural capital. Your morning routine, for instance, might always look like this:

- Wake up at 6 a.m.
- Check e-mail.
- Put in contacts.
- MUST MAKE COFFEE!
- Drink coffee while checking e-mail and reading news.
- Make and eat breakfast.
- Load dishwasher.
- Take shower.
- Brush teeth, starting with the right lower quadrant.
- Get dressed.
- Check e-mail again.
- Start dishwasher.
- Leave for office.

This is structural capital, albeit simplified. Your morning would not be as smooth if you got dressed before you took a shower. It just would not make any sense for you to leave for the office and put your contact lenses in at the office.

Just like having a process for getting yourself out of the house, a company can use a process so that its systems run smoothly. Take my office. At my firm, we have something called Quadrant Planning, which is just one example of the structural capital we have created to guide our communications with clients. It also has a practical, quality promoting approach.

As its name implies, Quadrant Planning is a four-part process that we use when meeting with clients; planning their accounting, tax, financial, and legacy solutions; implementing these solutions; and then following-up to maintain or revise solutions.

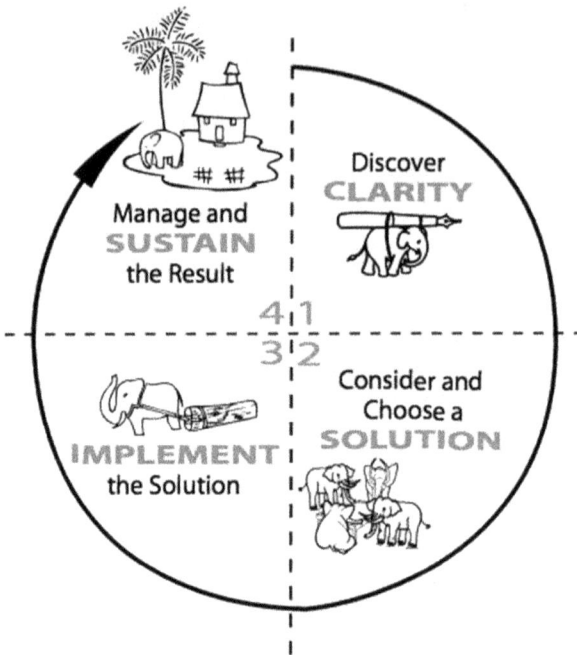

1. In Quadrant 1, Clarity, we examine a client's motives, consider his or her values, and create a vision that addresses the situation, leading a client to visual, clear, and ideal result.

2. In Quadrant 2, Solutions, we look at the steps necessary to reach the client's ideal result and clarified vision. We example available options and choose the one that is most efficient and effective. We communicate our approach and timeline to our client.

3. In Quadrant 3, Implementation, we implement the solution with the help of the client. Here, ongoing communication is crucial.

4. Finally, in Quadrant 4, Sustainability, we preserve a plan, change it if necessary, or address new needs over time, making sure that clarity is retained, solutions remain effective, and implementation continues.

Quadrant Planning, which was the focus of my book *Say Hello to the Elephants*, serves as the framework for our ongoing conversations with clients. Without the fourth phase of Quadrant Planning, for instance, we might forget to check in with our clients from time to time, particularly if our firm went through a particularly chaotic or stressful period. But if we ignored this final quadrant, our clients might forget why they engaged our firm in the first place. Or, their own goals from Quadrant 1 might change, and if our accounting and tax solutions do not change in accordance, we will become irrelevant.

In this way, the fourth phase of Quadrant Planning reminds us and forces us to check in with our clients. It is the single most important factor in retaining our clients. Without this structural capital, we would spend far too much time trying to find new clients as old clients walked out the door when their needs changed. We aren't always perfect in delivering each of the four quadrants, but this framework gives us a great target to work toward.

Build—and Rebuild—Relevant Structure

This brings me to an important point about structural capital: Any change in condition, whether internal or external, can require a company to change its structural processes. Not only do the strongest businesses build structures within their business, but they also reassess these structures to determine how relevant they are to the company's current needs. Too often, businesses create systems, and then they fail to examine whether these systems are meeting the company's current goals.

The Capitals and Me

If you ever hear yourself saying, "I have always done it that way," immediately ask yourself: "Why?"

As I write this chapter, for instance, I have 637 e-mails in my inbox. All of these e-mails, and more, were sitting in my inbox when I returned from a two-week vacation. Upon returning, I tended first and foremost to e-mails that were from clients or from other professionals who might be assisting my clients (financial planners and the like). But even after reading and addressing all these e-mails, I am still left with 637 e-mails. Try as I might, I cannot reduce my inbox below this number, despite the fact that I have been back from vacation for three weeks.

For the past five years, I have had a system for dealing with e-mails, which kept my inbox relatively clean. But now, something is clearly failing in my structural process with regard to my e-mail. I have only a vague idea of what remains in my inbox. Did a trusted colleague refer a client to me? Is a family member or friend waiting on an answer from me? I sure hope not, but without a system to truly address these e-mails, I cannot know for sure.

Clearly, I need to modify my system.

And it bears noting that my system is not inherently flawed, other than that it is not currently working for me. In the past, I have always categorized my e-mails based on when I need to address them. If an airline confirmation for travel scheduled in October enters my inbox, I immediately move the reservation to a folder labeled "October." If a client e-mails me with an urgent need, I put the e-mail in my "now" folder, which I address at the end of each day.

Theoretically, it's a great system, one that worked for five years.

A service provider of mine has another system. He trains his clients to label the subject of their e-mails with the action item and the due date. If I sent an e-mail requesting that we speak, the subject might be: Call Tony Rose anytime on Friday.

His argument on behalf of this system is that this allows him to see, at a glance, which e-mails need to be addressed immediately. The subject line of his incoming e-mails represents items that are added to his to-do list, which he can scan at any point during the day. He doesn't need to open each e-mail to determine whether the e-mails can wait or whether they require immediate attention. He also knows approximately how long the response to each e-mail can take, so he can manage his time appropriately, answering the easy e-mails before heading out the door to take his children to school and saving the more complicated responses when he has more time.

Neither system is better than the other, unless they stop working. Reflect back, for instance, on Webvan's defeat. Although Webvan's rapid expansion was not its most noteworthy structural flaw, perhaps the company could have been saved had it grown more slowly, giving it time to correct its major structural flaws before expanding to other areas.

And yet, rapid expansion works for other companies. In only five years Chobani became a billion-dollar business and a revolutionary force in the yogurt industry.

Before Chobani hit store shelves, Greek yogurt was almost nonexistent in the United States, with a meager 0.2 percent share of the yogurt category. Greek yogurt is high quality, all-natural, and has more protein than traditional yogurt.

Five years later, this yogurt accounted for 50 percent of U.S. yogurt sales.

And Chobani held greater than 50 percent share of the Greek yogurt market.

Chobani became the No.1 selling yogurt brand in the United States, outselling established giants like Dannon and Yoplait, in large part because of its structural capital.

Chobani's success has been dramatic, and intellectual capital in the form of an innovative product has obviously played a critical role. Founder and CEO, Hamdi Ulukaya, hired a friend and master yogurt-maker form Turkey to develop a recipe for Green yogurt, which was virtually unknown in the United States.

But the intellectual capital that was perhaps more important than the yogurt recipe was Ulukaya's knowledge of how popular Greek yogurt was in other parts of the world. His knowledge gave him the confidence to expand rapidly, using a process not typical in the start-up world.

Start-up companies that launch new food products typically expand slowly, starting in just a few markets. They often use co-packers to manufacture the product, rather than investing in production facilities. The goal is to develop a market share and brand presence just big enough to attract one of the major food conglomerates. If all goes well, the larger company will acquire the start-up and then use its existing manufacturing capacity, distribution network, and financial resources to mass produce, market, and sell the new product across the country.

But Hamdi Ulukaya's process was different. His structural capital was unique. Ulukaya bought a shuttered plant in 2005 before he even had a recipe for yogurt. He took control of the manufacturing process rather than outsourcing it to co-packers. And he priced Chobani based on what his costs would be when he was running at full capacity, not based on higher start-up costs. Basically, his structural capital was to go big—and fast.

"No start-up has done it any other way, so I wanted to do it another way. I bet on these guys being lazy, that they're not going to wake up that fast, and I said, *I'm going to be fast*"(Durisin 2013).

Ulukaya knew Greek yogurt was at a tipping point, and he set up a structure that embraced this.

Chobani yogurt was an instant hit with consumers, and because of its structural capital, the company was able to keep up with consumer demand. And Chobani continues to challenge conventional process. Chobani opened its second plant in December 2012, again in record-breaking fashion. The plant was built in only 326 days (a standard construction cycle is over two years), and is the largest yogurt manufacturing plant in the world. In fact, the factory was named "Plant of the Year" by *Food Engineering*.

Now, Chobani has assumed leadership of the entire Greek yogurt industry, working with Congress to ask the U.S. Department of Agriculture to recognize the nutritional value of Greek yogurt so that it can be included in school lunch programs.

Many start-up companies have developed innovative products, only to be swallowed up or crushed by their much larger competitors. Ulukaya succeeded where others failed because he took a risk and used an innovative process to take Green yogurt to the masses.

It bears noting, now, that where Chobani succeeded, Webvan failed. Like Chobani, Webvan grew big and fast, but this structure did not work for Webvan. Here is my analysis of why it failed: Webvan either ignored or paid too little attention to creating volume.

Webvan seemed to believe that "If you build it, they will come."

When they did not come in San Francisco, Webvan kept growing and pouring money into an admittedly amazing logistical solution. Had Webvan spent as much time considering their structures for acquiring customers, it might have identified the need to focus all efforts on areas of concentrated population. Had it coupled this focus with its terrific logistics, Webvan might be here today.

Chobani, on the other hand, had evidence that suggested its product would be a big hit. It not only grew physically, but also acquired new customers as it ramped up its physical structure.

The point is: Unlike financial capital, which is measured by objective numbers, the richness of a company's structural capital is measured by how well it supports a company.

This is especially important to note in entrepreneurial businesses. At the onset of a new business, an entrepreneur might be hands-on with most areas of the business. In the beginning, this serves the business well because the entrepreneur can quickly react to new opportunities and change its direction as these opportunities arise.

As it grows out of its start-up phase, what would happen if the entrepreneur remained actively involved in every single part of the business? One word comes to mind: micro-management. In an attempt to stay in control, the entrepreneur would, in fact, create the opposite result. As the business expanded, this early nimbleness would create havoc as the organization grew to need detailed systems for governance, documented handbooks that held institutional memory, and set-in-stone procedures for managing accounts payable and accounts receivable.

And herein lies the problem with implementing structural capital, especially for entrepreneurs. Many entrepreneurs are not process-oriented. In fact, one could argue that entrepreneurs have done everything within their power to defeat procedures, systems, and schedules. Entrepreneurs, in particular, crave spontaneity, flexibility, and newness. This characteristic is one that allows them to be successful, yet it can also plant the seed for defeat. The truth is that something that is heavy and large must be supported by structure. Without a framework, the best material in the world will come crashing down.

This is not to say that an entrepreneur or businessperson must abandon his or her values of freedom or newness and replace them with boring, stale processes. Rather, it means that an entrepreneur or business owner who wants rich structural capital must make decisions about the kinds of structure in place. Depending on the owner's values, the structure could be loose or rigid. Neither is necessarily correct, so long as it support the framework of your company.

Let us take a look at, for instance, a young company's approach to human resource management. Small organizations often make human resources decisions based upon the values of the owners. Hiring is a personal affair, and key managers don't have a refined hiring or retention process. In fact, hiring, retention, and promotion protocol would feel like overkill in a small business. Promotions and work rules generally are created one by one and based upon the relationship between the owner and his or her employees. The minutia of labor laws is often disregarded.

As a company grows, though, so does its employee population. Its personal touch, then, is understandably lost. This is where problems begin. The employees feel divided from the owner, so their loyalty is no longer enough to cause them to turn a blind eye to breaches of labor law. Predictably, many companies are hit with employee lawsuits as they begin to grow. This drains profits and, if the company survives, it reemerges with refined human resources solutions that support the larger company.

Keep in mind that even where there is no intentional structure, there is still structure—it is probably just a poor structure. If you do not make decisions and create systems for enforcing these decisions, your employees, clients, or vendors will do it on your behalf. They will be outside of your control, and not necessarily in the best interest of your company or your values.

Consider, for instance, the many employers who stop paying payroll taxes in order to use that money to pay other obligations. At first, they pay penalties and interest, but nothing really bad happens, so the company keeps failing to pay its payroll taxes. Eventually, though, the government will come after every single executive in the company. Liens are placed on executives' homes and bank accounts. This information not only scares the owners and executives, but it also degrades the creditworthiness of an organization—all because the company failed to implement a structure that supported the business's need to pay payroll taxes.

The Capitals and Me

Think back to your years in high school and college. Imagine that you were a "C" student all around. If you didn't change your methodology for studying, would you still be a "C" student the following semester?

You sure would be.

Now think about how often you arrive to appointments on time. If you always have been a late arriver, you always will be tardy unless you change your process for getting out of the door on time.

What about getting a job? If you constantly hit the computer want ads, but your applications are rejected, you need a different process for networking and finding a job.

All of these processes play into your structural capital.

Structural capital has three huge benefits:

1. First, it demands consistency. Systematic processes ensure that nothing within your organization is done haphazardly.
2. Second, if a systematic process is efficient, it alleviates an organization from having to reinvent the wheel each time it secures a new client, or delivers a product to a new customer.
3. But perhaps most importantly, when considered thoughtfully, structural capital can force an organization to focus on all four of the other capitals. A company can begin seeing how it might increase leads, for instance, by enriching its social capital. It can create a system for systematically evaluating each line item on its profit and loss statements to find less expensive but more efficient methods of creating its product. It can create systematic review and feedback procedures to evaluate its human capital, and it can also create processes to identify external factors that could encroach on its intellectual capital. These are just a few examples. The point to remember is that an organization can build strength by examining each link in the chain that delivers value to its customers.

So what kind of processes should a business consider?

Outside Processes

First comes outside processes, which describe the way you deliver value to your customers. I call them outside structures, because they are the processes that your customer can see—they are walking about outside, visible to the naked eye.

Think of outside processes like the way FedEx delivers a package, particularly in comparison to the United States Postal Services (USPS). The outside structure for FedEx is far superior to the outside structure for

USPS. FedEx has shorter lines, greater online capabilities, cheaper rates for business customers, more reliable delivery times, and happier personnel.

The USPS has none of those.

Here are some outside processes to consider:

- Pay close attention to your own communication models, which represent an outside process. You could be the smartest person in the room with the best and most valuable process, but if you are tangential, provide too much information, or use lingo that the customer cannot understand, your customers will be unable to sort through the debris. With desperation, their minds will start trying to grab onto something, but your words will be akin to a subway entering a tunnel and never stopping.
- Be disciplined about your processes for using social media. Consider how this impacts your customers' perception of you and your product or service.
- Think about how your customers communicate back and forth with you. Does this process work smoothly?
- What about the process for delivering your product or service to your clients?
- Take a look at how you solicit product feedback. Is it effective? Do you do it at all?
- Explore your communication models. This topic alone could fill volumes and volumes of books, so I will offer just two pointers: Keep it honest, and keep it simple.

Inside Processes

Unlike these outside processes, inside processes occur backstage. These are the processes that the clients will never see, yet if they are inefficient, they will manifest through poor service or substandard products.

I was flying through San Francisco a couple of days after the Korean Air crash, and I suspected that there was a high probability that my flight would be canceled or rerouted. I kept checking the flight status, and the airline's website regularly assured me that my 9 a.m. flight would be departing on time.

When I fell asleep at 10 p.m. the night before the trip, the flight was still being listed as an on time departure. Somewhere around 11 p.m., when I was fast asleep, the airline sent me an e-mail letting me know that the flight had been postponed by a day. So when I awoke at 6 a.m., I learned that my flight was now scheduled to be in the air at the same time as the meeting I was traveling to attend.

Clearly, this was not going to work for me.

Of course, the first thing I did was hop on the phone and attempt to contact the airline and find out what my options were. I was unable to get through for hours because every other person flying through San Francisco was also calling the airline. When I finally did reach a customer service representative, I was met with a gruff apology.

And that was the extent of the representative's empathy. I explained that I lived close to several other airports, and I asked if he could find a spot for me on one of the airline's planes leaving from a different airport and flying through a city other than San Francisco.

The airline representative told me he was unable to fly me out of a different airport. It was not in his power to make this change.

It cost me a lot of money, but I ended up calling a different airline entirely, driving to a different airport, and catching another flight.

I imagine that the original airline's inside processes were designed with some end goal in mind. Surely, they knew before 11 p.m. that the flight would be canceled. Even if they did not know, surely they could have found another solution for the people affected by the flight changes. Perhaps the airline did not believe it should empower its employees, or perhaps it wanted to protect its employees by consolidating the amount of time they would deal with unhappy customers, so it saved the notice until the middle of the night. Regardless, the internal processes that guided the airline's communication models resulted in me feeling frustrated and dissatisfied.

If I am given a choice, I will never fly that airline again.

Compare this to my experience on yet another airline, JetBlue. During another trip of mine, JetBlue delayed one leg of my flight due to poor weather conditions. Shortly after the delay was announced, the pilot walked through the gate with a weather map describing to passengers exactly what was happening that was causing weather concerns. At the same time, a flight attendant set up a buffet table, and loaded it with water, peanuts, pretzels, and soda. Admittedly, the spread was not impressive by most definitions, but we were so impressed with the airline's genuine concern for our well-being that it might as well have been serving filet mignon.

In this case, the internal processes that guided the airline's communication models manifested in a positive way. Every passenger on that flight, who eventually did leave the terminal, knew that this airline valued its customers, first and foremost. (This happened over 10 years ago, and I'm still talking about it today. Props to JetBlue!)

Your Processes and Your Values

This brings me to an important point: Your processes—whether they are inside or outside—are a reflection of your values. If you value your customers, your processes will reflect this, and so will your bottom line. If you place your customers too far down the list, though, you will eventually lose your customers, and your revenue will drop.

So do not create systems just for the sake of creating systems. Create structures that have meaning and that truly serve your customers and, therefore, your bottom line.

Beware, too, of processes that make people feel important but do not truly contribute value to the customer or client.

That is not to say that you should cut off essential accountability steps that help you understand whether you are progressing or not. We require our office assistants to write down what they are doing, even though they might not be devoting time that is directly tied to creating value for the client. However, this system does hold our assistants accountable for how they are spending their time, which means they are much more likely to spend their time supporting the firm. And this *does* create value for the clients down the line.

You see, as always, your organization's human capital (i.e., your organization's values) will bleed into everything you do—including the structures you create. If you value your clients, the structures should be established to facilitate your clients' lives.

If you build structures based on bad values, on the other hand, you might as well join General George Armstrong Custer at the Battle of the

Bighorn. As you might remember from history class, Custer was a cavalry commander and Civil War hero during the American Indian Wars in the late 1800s. On the morning of June 25, 1876, Custer led his men into battle against the Lakota Sioux and Northern Cheyenne Native Americans.

He had been ordered to wait for reinforcements at the mouth of the Little Big Horn River, but Custer wanted to make a name for himself, so he ignored orders and attacked. Less than an hour later, Custer had lost 265 of his soldiers, as well as his own life.

And all because he based his plans on bad values—on his own ego and his quest for personal glory. Instead of following the appropriate process, Custer decided to disobey orders because he was a grandstander. He took his men on a mission that ended in a massacre.

So how do you make sure that your structural capital is built with intention, and with your top values in mind? Start by remembering that any business is a chain of interrelated processes. Then:

1. Ask yourself this question: *Do these processes contribute to making a profit?*

   You might find that you do things a certain way for no reason other than that this is the way you have already done them. If a habit serves no purpose but to feed itself, replace it with something intentional.

2. Measure the satisfaction of your social capital constituents. If your customers, employees, and vendors are happy with your services, your structural capital is likely working, but remember to go deep. There are always things you could be doing better, so ask each segment of your social capital if there are things that your company could do to enhance your services.

   One way to do this is by sending an e-mail asking your social capital constituents to complete an anonymous online survey. Following are a few general questions that you might ask, but remember that I think you should go deep by asking detailed questions that are specific to your processes and company.

   - On a scale of 1 to 10, how much do you think ABC Company cares about its clients?
   - Which, if any, of our processes do you find cumbersome or frustrating?

- Which of the following methods of communication could we improve upon?
  - o Returning e-mails in a timely manner.
  - o Directing incoming phone calls to the appropriate department.
  - o Invoicing.

  Although you should go deep with your surveys, keep them short so that your clients need to spend only four or five minutes giving you feedback. You can send a new survey every month or two, constantly soliciting feedback about the different processes, services, or products that your company has established.

3. For each process, ask the question: "Does this process facilitate or impede delivering value to our constituents?" Remember that there are certain measurable—like profits, satisfaction ratings, turnover, and the like—that can assess if a process is effective. Be bold and use these as measuring sticks.

Finally, and most importantly, never be afraid to modify or fine-tune a system. Changing a structure is uncomfortable, simply because it challenges you to operate outside your comfort zone. Strengthening a structure is like strengthening a muscle—it hurts at first, but it will give you and your company more longevity and the ability to carry more workload in the long run.

CHAPTER 4

Intellectual Capital

We all know stuff. If you are a service provider, you know your industry. If you are in sales, manufacturing, or distribution, you are likely well familiar with your product. Indeed, a company would not be in business if it did not turn some sort of knowledge into intellectual capital.

But knowing stuff alone is not enough to constitute *rich* intellectual capital. I know a good deal about golf, for instance, but I have never used this knowledge, or any derivative of it, to further my professional career. I also know a good deal about tax code, but this knowledge does not make me stand out from the other certified public accounting firms in Los Angeles and Las Vegas. The most powerful intellectual capital represents several subsets of knowledge that are carefully packaged in a way that make a company's product or service difficult to duplicate. For instance, I also know about values-based planning, which is seemingly unrelated to accountancy. But I have used this knowledge to make my accountancy firm more distinguishable from my competitors.

More often than not, when we are preparing taxes for a client, we attempt to understand both the values and conative make-up of our client. This helps us provide a context for our advice, and we shine when presenting information to these leaders because we effectively tap into their goals and natural wiring.

This is not to say that a company's knowledge itself must be unique. Every single thing that you know, even if you think it is trivial, could be important in building your company's intellectual capital. Instagram, for instance, got started by two guys who had no financial capital. They took photography, technology, and aesthetics—none of which were unique pieces of knowledge—and they developed an application that is now used worldwide.

What makes Instagram rich in intellectual capital is that its founders coupled photography, technology, and aesthetics with the power of social media networking. The app is used by a robust network of connected social media users who are not likely to jump ship, abandon their followers or followees, and discard their history.

All of these subsets of knowledge—photography, technology, aesthetics, and social media—chip away at a competitor's ability to steal market share.

Almost always, companies offer a product or service that can be closely replicated, and this opens the door to competition and erodes the company's potential. Such intellectual capital is not particularly powerful because it is traded as a commodity. For instance, if you walk into a major drugstore or discount retail store, you will see rows and rows of men's deodorant packaged in dark, manly looking colors. The rows of women's deodorant will be packaged in softer colors, appealing to a more feminine crowd. Some people may have a brand preference, but the different brands of deodorant are all treated as commodities. For all intents and purposes, deodorant is deodorant.

Years ago, smart marketing companies created aerosol deodorant for men, and clear deodorant for women, thus eliminating the clumps of white deodorant under their armpits. For a while, this intellectual capital gave these companies an advantage, but competitive brands soon replicated the innovations in deodorant, and men's and women's deodorant became a commodity once again.

Creating powerful intellectual capital means that you de-commoditize your product or service, which is easier said than done. You can do this one of two ways:

1. By adding knowledge to make a product or service unique.
2. By turning human, social, or structural capitals into intellectual capital.

Adding Knowledge to Create Unique Intellectual Capital

The first way to de-commoditize your product or service is to pile more intellectual capital on top of existing intellectual capital.

What if a deodorant company merged with a pharmaceutical company and figured out how to add vitamins and supplements to its product so that deodorant absorbed into bodies and provided things like weight loss, birth control, testosterone, vitamin B, or calcium? This is what I mean by adding knowledge to make a product or service less inimitable.

Consider, for instance, Uber. If you live in a major city, you might know about Uber. Launched in San Francisco in 2009, Uber began as a limo timeshare of sorts among friends, but it soon grew into something much bigger. Uber's founders created a smartphone app that could dispatch a car-for-hire at the touch of a button. The Uber app essentially generated real-time leads for the myriad of self-employed limo drivers and livery service businesses that were already in existence. Passengers, in exchange, are able to locate an Uber car on their smartphone, send for it, and then receive real-time updates letting the passenger know exactly where the car is, when it will arrive, what the driver's name is, the license plate of the car, and the make and model of the Uber car that is being sent.

Between December 2013 and April 2014, Uber doubled the number of cities in which it had cars operating—from about 50 to more than 100. It has plans to expand to the 500 largest cities worldwide. The company raised more than $300 million in capital from big-name investors to fund their expansion. And Uber's valuation at the end of 2013 was estimated at almost $4 billion.

Perhaps the strongest evidence of Uber's success was the reaction from competitors, specifically the taxi industry, who fought to put up legal roadblocks in several cities.

So how did Uber shake up an industry that is as old as the car itself in just a few short years? The founders of Uber identified an inefficient model, restructured it, and harnessed intellectual capital to improve it.

Prior to Uber's entrance into the market, two basic models existed in the ride-for-hire industry: limo services, which were expensive and not available on demand; and taxi services, which are often inefficient.

From the rider's perspective, taxi rides are terribly unreliable: There is no guarantee that a taxi will be available when needed. From the driver's perspective, business is inconsistent. It is difficult to predict demand, and even when the driver picks up a fare in one direction, there is no guarantee that the driver will be able to pick up a fare on the way back. Dead return trips are expensive for drivers, especially since fares are regulated and cannot be increased to compensate for dead time. Drivers earn low wages and because they carry cash, they are vulnerable to robbery.

One cause of the inefficiencies is the heavy regulation of fares in the taxi industry, often in place for good reason—to protect the consumer. But there is also just the simple logistical problem of matching supply (drivers) to demand (would-be passengers) in real time.

Calling a taxi, then, is always a big unknown. Will it arrive in five minutes or 35 minutes?

Enter Uber. Uber started by building structural capital that addresses deficiencies in the ride-for-hire industry, but its true power was adding intellectual capital that the taxi and limo industries do not have.

First, Uber transformed the ride-for-hire structure. Passengers no longer have to make reservations in advance or stand at a curb waving down a taxi. They can summon a car with a tap on their smartphone. The app eliminates uncertainty: Potential passengers are immediately informed where the closest Uber affiliated car is located, how long it will take for the car to arrive, and how much the trip will cost. Payment is made automatically through the passenger's registered credit card, which eliminates the need for cash. This is both a convenience for passengers and a safety feature and payment guarantee for drivers. Receipts are then e-mailed to the passengers' smartphones.

The strategic use of structural capital alone made Uber a fierce competitor, but what made the Uber app truly revolutionary was the intellectual capital that was added to the company.

Even with an innovative structure, the app could not be successful if cars were not available when and where passengers needed them, so Uber employed statisticians to develop algorithms that predicted traffic flow. The statisticians identified traffic patterns at the neighborhood level, allowing Uber to predict what direction, times, and areas people moved in. Drivers are now armed with this intellectual capital so they know when and where to linger. The more data Uber collects, the more precise it becomes with demand forecasts, and the faster it can connect cars and passengers. Cars typically arrive no later than 15 minutes after an order is placed. Regardless, prior to calling an

Uber car, passengers can tell how far out the cars are, planning their car-for-hire needs accordingly.

Uber uses this intellectual capital to develop a dynamic or surge pricing model, meaning fares vary based on demand. When the demand for drivers increases, fares automatically increase, incentivizing more drivers and discouraging passengers who are unwilling to pay the higher rates. If demand exceeds supply, prices increase until equilibrium is reached.

Intellectual capital is the key to Uber's success, but Uber's founders didn't necessarily have the intellectual capital personally to make their vision a reality, but they hired engineers and statisticians who did, and applied that capital to restructure the drive-for-hire industry. The data Uber collects becomes the company's own proprietary intellectual capital, stacking more knowledge on top of existing knowledge, and providing Uber with a competitive edge over existing and aspiring competitors.

As successful as Uber is, it bears noting that it has competitors like Lyft that are challenging it to keep evolving. In fact, even Uber's own robust intellectual capital is not complete. Another emerging app, Bandwagon, pairs people who want to reach the same destination at a lower fare. Let's say that both George and Randy are going to the airport, and they live within a few miles of each other. Bandwagon pairs them up, which allows them to take the same taxi or Uber car and share the fare. Whether Bandwagon will have the same success as Uber is still unknown, but one thing is for sure: Intellectual capital can always be improved upon.

If Uber is a shining example of adding intellectual capital to make an existing service or product better, Sony is an example of what not to do. Once a giant in consumer electronics, Sony failed to strengthen its position in the market by missing its chance to capitalize on intellectual capital that could have allowed it to maintain its market share.

Sony Corporation has a long, storied history of innovation and rich intellectual capital. The company was truly a pioneer in consumer electronics. It developed and marketed the first commercial transistor radio in the 1950s, the revolutionary Trinitron color TV and Walkman in the 1970s, the world's first CD player in the 1980s, and home computers and the popular Playstation in the 1990s.

For decades, Sony was synonymous with innovation and technical achievement.

In the past couple decades, though, Sony's businesses and brand have been in decline, eclipsed by competitors like Samsung and Apple, who gained market share in many of the key consumer electronic categories in which Sony competed. Sony posted losses for the past several years, and a string of new CEOs have been engaged in an uphill battle to revive the company.

The turning point for Sony was, perhaps, the company's failure to capitalize on the intellectual capital it possessed in digital technology. Sony had technology to create a digital music player, as well as a catalog of music, more than a decade before Apple introduced the iPod.

Indeed, the concept was floated by Sony in the 1980s, and the iPod wasn't released until 2001. Imagine what would have become of Sony if it has released a digital music player back in the 1980s!

Yet, Sony missed this opportunity. Competing divisions, scattered resources, and an insistence on proprietary formats hindered this innovation. Specifically, engineering divisions did not want to be led by media divisions. Media divisions did not want consumers to download music in a way that would undercut relationships and contracts with recording artists.

Years later, when Sony was playing catch up to competitors in the digital music arena, the company resisted using the MP3 standard format, instead introducing proprietary files that were cumbersome for the consumer. Essentially, the company's poor structural and human capital hindered it from using its intellectual capital, allowing competitors to get a foothold.

Sony illustrates that intellectual capital can become a commodity even in an industry that is driven by technical breakthrough. The advantage gained from technical superiority has a limited life; eventually competitors introduce substitutes or even leapfrog existing technology with superior replacements.

Despite its deep talent and knowledge pool, Sony did not add intellectual capital, thereby failing to innovate at the pace of its competitors. And even worse, Sony neglected to strengthen its intellectual capital with social or human capital.

The failure is perhaps best understood in contrast to Apple, a company with an almost cult-like following.

Unlike Sony, Apple excelled in augmenting its intellectual capital by understanding its consumers and defining its set of values (human capital).

While Sony was struggling to keep up, Apple's capitals were in a virtuous cycle: The company used intellectual capital to innovate, which strengthened its brand image and reinforced its human capital, ultimately building a relationship with consumers (social capital). Apple's technology was not always superior to its competitors, but its human capital and resulting social capital made the company to stand out.

Sony failed to build the same kind of brand loyalty outside of Japan. The company seemed to have had difficulty understanding consumers and anticipating or imagining how they might use its cutting edge technology. Although often technically superior to its competitors, Sony's proprietary formats, complicated interfaces, and premium pricing for features that were not important to the mass market weakened its products. Sony ended up in a vicious cycle. Its lack of product introductions that resonated with consumers tarnished its once stellar brand image and weakened its relationship with consumers.

Turning Other Capitals Into Intellectual Capital

Uber is a great example of adding additional knowledge to strengthen a company's position in a market, and it also serves as an example of turning another capital—in this case, structural capital—into intellectual capital. Its structural capital is the robust Uber app, and its intellectual capital would not be distinct without this structure.

In the technology age, examples abound of companies who have added infrastructure (structural capital) to make their intellectual capital distinct. Instagram did it. In fact, the same year that Kodak entered bankruptcy, Instagram sold to Facebook for $1 billion—all because Instagram cornered the photography-app market first.

For all intents and purposes, Netflix put mega-giant Blockbuster out of business by adding technology to the experience of renting movies.

As a child, a friend of a friend spent a ton of time in her mom's court-reporting agency. As an adult, she worked in the technology industry. One day, though, she was visiting her mom at the court-reporting agency and overheard some of the employees complain about the way court reporters are scheduled.

An idea was born. My friend's friend realized that the court-reporting world needed a software program that matched court reporters with law firms. This way, law firms could secure court reports for their depositions without picking up a phone.

Although it is the easiest to spot, structural capital is not the only way to strengthen intellectual capital. Christian bookstores, for instance, have the same knowledge as regular bookstores, but they have used their human capital (their Christian value set) to appeal to a specific group of people.

Virtual currency is another product that is defined as much by its social capital as its intellectual capital. If you are a computer geek (a term used here with great admiration—and even some amount of jealousy!), and you and your gadget friends are talking to each other about the latest and greatest, what can be better than creating crypto-currency that only you and your fellow tech-geeks can understand? Virtual currency took off because it leveraged social capital and gave tech-geeks instant credibility and instant prestige. If an investor wants to keep abreast of market trends, the only way to purchase virtual currency, and the only want to under-stand them, is to ask a computer geek. In a way, the intellectual, financial, and social capital represented by virtual currency is its own revenge of the nerds.

Speaking of nerds, when I became an accountant, I prepared tax returns. To my employer, I was a commodity. My employer could have replaced me with another young accountant. But soon, I realized that I had a way of preparing and delivering tax returns that made me unique. In fact, for me, being an accountant has never been about delivering tax returns and creating financial statements. Yes, those are important, but that is not why I am unique.

My clients come to me because I want to solve problems. More than helping my clients address their tax needs, I like helping them solve their problems—whether financial, structural, intellectual, social, or human. When my clients and I are meeting to discuss financial issues, I regularly address issues outside the scope of the traditional account-ant's duties. I have used both my social capital and my human capital to de-commoditize myself. My clients do not hire me to prepare a tax return. They hire me because my human capital and my values have become part of my intellectual capital. My clients know we will have a long-term relationship.

In a service business, very few people think through and can verbalize what creates the differentiator. If your clients come to you just to prepare the service, you are providing a commodity. But if you can identify the reason they come to *you* specifically, your intellectual capital may have been strengthened by some other capital.

I hire a specific editor to tighten up my books. She knows about writing and grammar, but wouldn't *any* editor know about writing and grammar? I hire my editor because she can transfer my voice into black and white.

Strengthening Your Intellectual Capital

If you have customers or clients, you have a product or service that is already solving problems. But have you defined it so that you can replicate it as you grow and expand? It took me 10 years to realize that I focus more on relationships than I do on tax returns, and once I realized this, I became much more efficient when training my firm's tax preparers. I will not put a tax preparer in a room with a client unless that preparer is a people person. Doing so would degrade my intellectual capital.

When it comes to fully pinpointing your intellectual capital, the questions you must be able to answer are the following:

- *What is the value that I deliver?* Figure out why your customers are coming back.

Then, strengthen your intellectual capital even more by asking:

- *How can I apply my human capital to make my product or service less inimitable?*
- *How can I enhance my social capital so that my intellectual capital is strengthened?*
- *How can I change the structure of my business so that the intellectual capital is strengthened?* This might mean creating

technology around your product or service, or it might mean building a method of communicating that makes your client feel more secure.

- Then, finally, ask: *What knowledge can I add to my product or service to make it less inimitable?* For this, start by identifying your intellectual capital. Write down as many things that you know as possible. These might be things like: How to fix a car, how to shop online, or how to use Instagram.

Ready, set, go:

The Capitals and Me

What Do I Know?

I did this exercise with a group of graduate students who wrote things like:

- Tie my shoes
- Drive a car
- Speak Mandarin
- Cook
- Ride a bike
- CPR
- Deliver a baby
- Paint nails

The value of many of these is obvious: CPR, speaking Mandarin, and cooking. I suppose that knowing how to deliver a baby could come in handy about 251 times a minute.

Some are less obvious, but I argue that they are equally important. When I was a very young (and handsome) student at the University of Southern California, I was newly married, taking 16 units per semester, and working 36 hours a week in a men's shoe store.

I tied a lot of shoes. I would run from campus into Van Nuys, and I would shine 30 pairs of shoes a day and tie shoes for a living. I made money doing that, so knowing how to tie shoes benefited me. That was part of my intellectual capital.

One of my clients is a national limousine company that services Florida, New York, and Los Angeles. You bet knowing how to drive a car has value.

One of my colleagues and I have friends who created a company that allows a person to pick up a bike in one place and leave it somewhere else, so I argue that knowing how to ride a bike also has value.

And all over town are cottage businesses of people making a ton of money painting nails and toes.

I am reminded here of Steve Job's famous commencement speech about connecting the dots. Perhaps one of his main themes is that when you aware that what you know is special, you can connect the dots when the opportunity presents itself.

Finally, remember that if you can name it, you can claim it. You could have the greatest process for figuring out a solution to life's problems, but if you cannot wrap it up with an emotionally appealing bow, no one will know what solution you provide. For instance, imagine flipping through the yellow pages to find a home healthcare agency to help you with your ailing parent. You are presented with options like Tony Rose's Homecare Services and A-to-Z Homecare. And then you spot: Visiting Angels Homecare. *This* is what you need—a company that will come into your home and be your angel.

CHAPTER 5

Financial Capital

When considering financial capital, a business owner might fall on one of two polar sides of a spectrum. On one end are the people who believe that money is the sole objective of owning a business. These people are driven exclusively by a profit motive. They care not what they sell; they care only that it is sold for money.

On the other end are those who believe that money is inconsequential. These people are driven by an emotional motive. They have their hearts and souls invested into a company. They care about the product or service and give no attention to its market value. Even if they do sell their product or service at value, they don't emphasize the company's health, leaving the business's health to pure luck.

In either extreme, the end result is always the same. A business owner with the sole intention of making money will be compensated eventually with a failing business. Although people in this camp might make a profit at the outset, leeches are always exposed for what they are. Ultimately, these con artists are driven into the ground by bad values, shoddy products and services, and small or nonexistent groups of people willing to lend a helping hand. In other words, these people lack the necessary human, intellectual, and social capital to sustain a business.

On the other side of the spectrum are the business owners who consider money to be inconsequential. These people fail to implement the proper systems for protecting and preserving their financial resources. Oftentimes, these business owners believe on some level that money is evil, so they simply ignore its existence. Although these business owners might also have an initial success, their inattention to financial capital is insufficient to support the company's long-term viability.

Now is a good time to explain what I mean by the term financial capital. Most of us think that financial capital is money. While money is a component of financial capital, financial capital also is comprised of tangible and intangible resources that the company owns, which could includes desks, chairs, equipment, cars, patents, trademarks, copyrights, and anything else that can be sold. The physical embodiment of a company, including a bank account and securities account, are the financial capital resources that a company can possess.

Other people, companies, and entities will always have claims on these resources. When you hire your team, you have to pay them. Even the most unsophisticated business owner knows that he or she must have a way to pay employees. No money tree is planted out back to pick when payroll time rolls around.

But there *is* a figurative money tree, and that money tree is your business. To reap the fruits of that tree, a business owner must have a structure in place to water the tree, pick the fruit, store that fruit, and protect it from scavengers.

Sick of the metaphor? Don't be. Too few businesses think it is important to keep their financial resources safe. They somehow think the money just happens.

Social, structural, human, and intellectual capital all work together to produce financial capital. In short, the capitals are the trees in your business orchard. When financial capital is considered within the context of this book, business owners begin to understand that financial capital is really lubrication that enables the other capitals to function. It is also a barometer for understanding how efficient a business has used and employed the other four capitals.

The Capitals and Me

Just like a business's financial capital cannot be considered in a vacuum, neither can an individual's financial capital. Your money is simply a tool for enriching the other capitals in your life. People who consider money to be the end-all and be-all find themselves dedicating their lives to their jobs. And they often find themselves without a network of friends (social capital), ignoring their own values (human capital), and disregarding the structural capital that would allow them to balance or integrate their personal lives and their professional lives. And often, they do this at the expense of unleashing the creative power that would build rich intellectual capital and allow them to find a more fulfilling career.

The best way to get a grasp on how your financial capital can be used to support your life is to work with your advisors—accountants and/or otherwise—to identify those tangible and intangible assets that you own. Once you understand what your assets do, how they grow, and what you can do to make them increase or decline, you can begin making positive and specific decisions about how to deploy them as a means of enriching your entire life.

Most people run away from budgets like they run away from wild animals, but if you do not sit down, consider your goals, and consider your resources, you will deploy your financial capital in ways that are willy-nilly instead of ways that are intended to provide you with more life satisfaction and a stronger integration of all the capitals that make you a rich person.

It becomes critical, then, to consider a company's financial health as a temperature gauge for the business. To be clear, though, I am not saying that financial capital should be considered an unmanageable byproduct. When financial capital is categorized as a derivative, a business is basically deciding to forego a critical part of its ability to influence positive outcomes—that is, how it protects, preserves, and deploys its financial capital.

Paul Higgins was an avid soccer enthusiast and an English native who knew how popular and important indoor soccer training was in other parts of the world. He had a sincere desire to support the sport he loved, and to introduce indoor soccer (or futsal) to his community. He and his business partner, Kevin Gilmore, built a 73,000-square-foot, state-of-the-art indoor soccer facility in Torrance, a large suburb of Los Angeles.

Futsal quickly became popular with soccer enthusiasts, both child and adult, and the facility became a welcome part of the community. In less than three years, Higgins had built a database of 28,000 players and regularly hosted 4,000 players each week.

But despite his intellectual capital, social capital, and authentic human capital, Higgins acknowledged that the facility was "undercapitalized and incurred regular operational losses" (Green 2012). Had he more time, he may have been able to make the business profitable, but the money ran out. As a testament to his labor of love, Higgins chose to sell the ongoing operation even though he acknowledged that he might have recouped more money had he closed the business and just sold off its assets. He felt he owed it to the soccer world to keep the facility open and was rightfully proud of his legacy to the sport.

In 2012, Higgins sold his futsal arena to AEG, the parent company of the Los Angeles Galaxy, which was bankrolled by billionaire Philip Anshutz.

The new owners brought some synergies to the business that enhanced its value. They could use the arena to promote the Los Angeles Galaxy team to local soccer fans, to hold practices, and to establish soccer training programs run by Galaxy staff and players. And critical to their success was that as they figured out how to rebrand, restructure, and improve their newly acquired business, they had the luxury of time that was afforded to them by a large, wide financial tarp.

Financial capital works not only as the output of human, intellectual, social, and structural capital, but also as the umbrella that protects these capitals during a down cycle. It works like this: The successful deployment of social, human, intellectual, and structural capitals creates a financial surplus that can work as an insurance policy during down cycles. But before it can become a surplus, this money must be given proper attention. In the case of Higgins' futsal arena, the money simply was not there early enough to give his human, intellectual, social, and structural capital wings.

I have a more personal example as well. Mark and Trent are some friends of mine who have developed a pretty great little aerospace company over the course of many years. Grossing around $15 million early in their venture, they self-financed their inventory, had strong receivables, and were able to stash a bit of cash in the bank. All of the equipment was paid in full. While sales had remained flat, they found themselves in an increasingly competitive environment. There was huge price pressure and their gross profits declined steadily. They bid on jobs accepting lower and lower pricing. As a result of the lowered pricing, Mark and Trent didn't blink twice when gross profits declined in tandem with the reduced profits.

They remained out of debt and were able to pay their bills, so neither of them paid great attention to their books. But last year, something happened that surprised them into action: Their gross profit dipped radically. They had to draw on their line of credit to pay their bills for the first time in 10 years. They also discovered that the inventory they thought they had, based on their electronic records, was incorrect. They actually had almost a half million dollars less in inventory.

It might be intuitive that lower prices will yield reduced financial resources, but this company's owners started paying attention to the erosion in their financial condition way, way late in the game. When they finally took a careful look at what was going on with their financial capital, they spotted the deficiency in the recording of inventory, and they realized that they had incorrectly priced some of their items.

With this new focus on the business's financial health, Mark and Trent were able to take immediate action to institute a better pricing model. They also made modifications to their recording and periodic monitoring of the inventory system.

Early results are promising, but it is too soon to tell whether they were able to right their ship in time, but one thing is certain: They could have caught the mistakes much earlier if they had both inquired about the eroding gross profit percentages in the first place.

A business owner cannot afford to ignore the economic cause and effect that happens within a business. If you don't implement a structure that allows you to understand the cause-and-effect scenarios on your balance sheet, someone else will implement a structure, and it might not be one that you approve of.

I see this firsthand when working with my clients. Businesses that are lacking in one of the capitals (perhaps they are lacking a structural capital that protects their financial leverage) will end up with a shortage of money. Banks seldom loan money to companies that have limited financial capital. Lacking financing, some cut corners by paying their employees, but not paying their payroll taxes. Eventually, and when it is least convenient, the Internal Revenue Service comes after these businesses, and in a big way. The government can seize assets, force divestiture, and hammer a nail into the coffin of an already suffering business. Because owners are personally liable for unpaid payroll taxes, the mess begins to consume the owners' personal financial capital as well.

On the other hand, businesses with sound financial capital can weather a down cycle by using financial capital as a tarp. Even if a business is not profitable for a short period of time, a business with a history of strong intellectual, structural, social, and human capital will not be forced to cut corners, compromise values, or put itself in harm's way because the financial capital generated by effective use of those capitals has created a sort of war chest for rainy days.

So how does a business protect its financial capital?

Lacking any other structure, most businesses evaluate past performances. That certainly is a good place to start. That said, historical records demonstrate trends and results, they are not an indication of a company's real-time health. Most business owners look at what happen*ed* and not what is happen*ing*. They fail to find a bridge that relates yesterday's temperature to today's temperature.

Although there are many solutions and countless books written on the subject of managing and tracking a business's financial health, I suggest using the following as a general guideline, filling in your holes in knowledge by reading books and hiring advisors:

1. Understand your historical records. This means that you know and understand the elements of your financial reports. While understanding the lines on your profit and loss statement is critical, so too is understanding how your expenses affect your profit, and understanding how different line items work to increase or decrease your bottom line. Understand trends, whether they are seasonal or directed by other outside forces. When you see something abnormal, don't be like Mark and Trent. Spend a bit of extra time to look deeper. Don't make assumptions and then end your discovery process. Work to gain a true understanding of the situation.

2. Know where you want to go, and how this relates to your financial numbers. If you see that your business has been moving further and further away from your goals, ask enough questions to understand why this has happened and what you can do to prevent it in the future. You might take a look at my first book, *Say Hello to*

the Elephants, which includes a good process for planning for the future.

3. Know your key performance indicators (KPIs), and know where they are every single day. KPIs are existing numbers or markers that can measure a business's success.

   You should identify three to five of these KPIs that tell you how your business is doing. Think of your KPIs like the charts or a gyroscope. Would you ever trust the captain of a ship who failed to read the charts and didn't know how to use a gyroscope? Of course not. Nor should you trust yourself to run your business if you have not identified and learned how to evaluate your KPIs.

   Whatever your KPIs are, and they are different for every company, they represent facts about the economy, an industry, or a company. Likely, you already have thought of metrics that tell you how your business is doing. For instance, when I started my business 40 years ago, I always measured my company's health based on the amount of money we received each day. Today, 40 years later, I still walk to the front desk most days and ask our front-desk receptionist, Jessica, how much money we have received on our receivables.

   What are those things that tell you how you are doing? Defining those metrics allows you to think through what changes in the numbers, either up or down, mean with regard to your five capitals.

   Know the current status of each of these KPIs by heart, but let me issue a word of warning: Don't go overboard here. Having more than a dozen is absolutely overkill in my estimation. Three to five generally covers the important bases. When you look at your numbers daily, weekly, monthly, and quarterly, you will begin to identify patterns and, perhaps more importantly spot deficiencies.

   So what are some examples of KPIs?

   KPIs can be lagging indicators or leading indicators. Lagging indicators report what happened in your business. For instance, a profit and loss statement is a lagging indicator. Lagging indicators do not change what happened, of course, but if they are used to forecast the future, they can change what you do in the future.

   Think of it like this: They say that insanity is behaving in the same way and expecting different results. If your business's results are disappointing, and you have a KPI that is a lagging indicator that your results are going to be the same in the future, you know that you cannot behave the same way and expect to see something different happen.

Leading indicators are those that have not yet converted to money yet. They still hold promise. For example, a company that sells a product can probably measure its forecast with some degree of accuracy by knowing the number of leads in a sales pipeline.

There is always cost to leads, and companies with lagging indicators as a KPI should pay attention to the amount of money it takes to buy mailing lists, spend time with potential clients, or otherwise secure the lead, as changes to this will also change the funnel.

4. Be willing to change the hard stuff. It is easy to change the inconsequential stuff, but the reality may be that there are huge changes that need to be made that you are simply unwilling to make because it will put you in state of equilibrium and discomfort. But refusing to make these changes will only take your company to mediocrity, at best.

It is true that this takes some thinking, and you might need to hire someone. We aren't telling people managing capitals should be managed alone. But the question is: Are you really willing to do what needs to be done? Do you have the resolve to make the changes that you know need to be made to improve your results and performance?

CHAPTER 6

Keeping Five Eyes on the Fence

In the book *Willful Blindness*, Margaret Heffernan submits that you have all the information you need about solving problems right in front of your nose. The trouble is that we are often willfully blind. We "ignore the obvious at our peril" (Heffernan 2011). Facts make us uncomfortable. Solutions seem too difficult. Disrupting the status quo seems so hard. Early signs of disasters are evident, but in an effort to make mediocre situations seem acceptable, our minds move to rationalize that which is obviously putting us in danger.

Think of the cuckold who blames his wife's continued indiscretions on the other men. To make sense of his wife's adultery, he creates scenarios that explain away her deceptions. *They seduced her when she was vulnerable*, his mind rationalizes, ignoring all of the obvious signs that his spouse will continue to break her vows.

This is the same willful blindness so many business owners use to deal with the shortcomings in their operations. Perhaps they have a feeling something is not properly working, and they might even know exactly what is wrong, but addressing these gaps seems too difficult and too uncomfortable. Many business owners subconsciously believe that if they open their eyes and address issues, they will simultaneously open Pandora's box. That is seldom as true as this fact: Doing nothing is the same thing as doing the wrong thing.

In my previous book, *Say Hello to the Elephants*, I explained that we all have problems in our businesses that we somehow ignore, despite the fact that those problems desperately need to be addressed to feel fulfilled and peaceful. It is my belief that these problems usually seem like financial problems, but they actually constitute problems in human, social, structural, or intellectual capital, which negatively affect the bottom line.

By identifying these elephants and saying hello, you can begin to address the problems.

Just by participating in this quest to understand the holes in the fence that surrounds your business, you have completed a worthy exercise because you have become introspective about the mechanisms you have in place relative to all the different capitals. You cannot close a gap without evaluating what is happening and what the components of this gap are.

And to be sure, your business does have gaps. Invariably, a business will fall short in some areas. There is no perfect business. Going forward, then, your job is to continue your journey to find and close these gaps.

Beware, though, of the inherent difficulty in considering your business's capitals. In this book, we have attempted to artificially cut the pie by looking at each of the capitals as standalone entities. Indeed, there are unique characteristics in each of the five capitals, but if you look critically at each of the five capitals, you will see that very often, if not always, they are inextricably inter-tangled. A flawed structural capital in regard to managing vendor invoices could harm your social capital. On the flip side, a remarkably efficient structural process might make up for some flaws in your intellectual capital.

So, while I encourage you to consider your five capitals as individual units, consider them also as a chain link fence, with each piece bonded to another in a crisscross of complexities.

This very theme arose during the writing of this book when Uber experienced some bad press. The company was accused of price gouging during a snowstorm in New York City, and then later on New Year's Eve.

Uber works like this: When demand is normal, or below average, riders pay the normal fare, but the company increases its fares when demand for Uber cars is high. They call it "surge pricing." The company defends its policy by saying that charging passengers more encourages more Uber drives to be on call, thereby meeting increased demand during inclement weather and on special occasions. Although Uber's app alerts would-be passengers of the increased rate, some riders feel taken advantage of when they are charged a higher-than-usual rate.

And yet, this book describes Uber's intellectual capital as cutting edge, so at the onset of the negative publicity for Uber, I sent my editor an e-mail that read: "Take a look at today's paper. Uber might have messed up its social capital."

"What's the problem?" she wrote back. "Your case study about Uber is in the intellectual capital section. Uber's intellectual capital is still solid, even if its social capital takes a temporary hit."

I understood her point, but something felt off, so I took a deeper look at the scenario. And then I realized this: A strong interplay exists between the good use of intellectual capital and a negative approach to social capital. If I were alerted by my Uber smartphone app that the rate would be two or three times the normal rate during a busy hour, I might decide that I do not want to take Uber, opting instead for a traditional taxi, or one of Uber's competitors like Lyft, which offers the same service but with a slightly different structure. After all, the increased rate might outweigh the convenience provided by the intellectual capital.

I sent an e-mail to my editor that included this: "The point of the book is not that a company can focus on one or two of the other capitals and get along. The real theme is that a business owner must keep five eyes on the issues of a company. Rich intellectual capital alone cannot protect a business anymore than any other singular capital can protect a business."

Think of it like the game Whac-A-Mole, the carnival game where the player is armed with a mallet. As a plastic mole pops up from one of the many holes, the player tries to pop the mole in the head with the mallet. As the game progresses, the moles begin popping up faster and faster, in random sequence. To get a perfect score, the player has to whack every mole.

Likewise, if a business owner is focusing his or her eyes on one and only one aspect, another aspect will probably rear its head. Even when due attention is given to many of your capitals, adjusting one sets something in motion related to another capital. This is why so many companies languish or fail when they hit a certain size: The bigger the company, the more complex it becomes to consider it as a whole. (Just ask Netflix.)

Yet, any attention or decisions focused on one capital should be quickly followed by an analysis of the impact that decision might have on the other capitals, whether it is positive or negative. A company that cuts its employees' hours to 29 per week in an effort to avoid paying increased insurance costs under the Affordable Care Act might find itself with an HR revolt that is much more damaging than the insurance cost. This is not to say that no company should cut its employees' hours, but rather that a company should look at its unique chain-link fence, consider the interplay between each of its capitals, and make decisions accordingly. For instance, consider the following:

1. You have placed so much emphasis on your existing relationships with your clients or customers (social capital) that you fail to put a structure in place to find new clients or customers.

2. You are so occupied with refining the process for delivering your existing product (structural capital) that you fail to develop new intellectual capital so that you can be competitive in the new marketplace. (If you want to know how important it is to stay abreast of developing trends, just ask copy stores that failed to understand the encroachment of FedEx. Or ask any corner bookstore, if you can find one.)

Creating the Evidence to Understand Your Gaps

If you can measure it, you can manage it. This is not a new idiom, but it is a time-tested one. Business owners use a lot of different tools to measure success or failure, but here are a few ideas to get you started measuring different subsets in each of the capitals.

- Whether your company is respecting its values as well as its employees' conation and intelligences can almost be sensed viscerally. Do your employees wear smiles? Do you feel happy coming to your place of work?

  Answers to the affirmative are a good indication that your business places a lot of emphasis on understanding and honoring human capital.

  If you are confronted by ethical issues all of the time, if your employees seem at odds with each other or with you, or if you have a cliquish, gossipy employee base, your human capital is probably lacking.

- Of course, there are also 360 Degree Surveys, employee satisfaction surveys, and employee turnover rates to assess the health of employees and effectiveness of leaders. Such tools represent an effort for these companies to create a tangible representation of their teams' feelings. Remember, though, that you should have a deep understanding of who your company is and who its employees are. This might include the following:

- ○ Completing the company value exercise described on pages 32–33.
- ○ Having each of your employees complete a Kolbe A index.
- ○ Reading *Multiple Intelligences*, assessing the different intelligences of your employees, and asking them to self-assess their intelligences.

At my accountancy firm, we have each employee's Kolbe listed on the directory. Every time I dial Jessica's extension, I am reminded that she works best with details and a sense of order and that she avoids chaos. By understanding each employee's conative traits, and then considering how these characteristics contribute to the success of the company, we have a better context for leading these people. This promotes our management of each member and team in ways that get us to economic goals.

- More than a few tools out there will help you assess how your structural capital is supporting your social capital with respect to clients or customers. How many new prospects do you have? How many clients refer business to you? How many inquiries do you get from your website?
- Remember, though, that looking at one number is not enough to truly oversee the entirety of your five capitals. If I spend $100,000 in marketing as part of a structural campaign to bring in my social capital constituents in the form of customers, and I get 100 new prospects, I have no idea whether this is a great return on investment or a lousy return on investment. Part of having solid structural capital is having a deep understanding of all of your numbers. By this, I mean that you should know the answers to questions like the following:
  - ○ How much does it cost your business to secure one client or customer? (This can be determined by comparing the number of new clients or customers you have secured with the amount you have spent in marketing.)

- ○ With respect to that average number, how do each of your marketing funnels compare? Is it much cheaper to secure clients from your website than from the radio?
- ○ What percentage of prospects do you close?
- ○ What is the cost-per-prospect?
- ○ How much is a new customer worth, on average?

I'm not suggesting that you take a guess at these answers. I submit that if you know these numbers by heart, and you know when they change, you will be in better position to see where the gaps exist. Imagine, for instance, that your company increased its prospects from 100 to 150 by changing its structural capital and social capital. You cannot tell whether those changes were worthwhile unless you know what percentage of prospects close, what the cost per prospect is, and how much each new client is worth. If you spent $50,000 to get 20 additional prospects, and you close 2 percent of your prospects, you spent $50,000 to secure one new client. If your clients are worth $100,000, this is great. If your clients are worth $1,000, you can consider abandoning the marketing platform, making changes to the system you use for closing clients, or otherwise repairing the gap.

- Read Chapter 5 again. The understanding of how financial capital is affected by the success and failures in your other four capitals might be found in the numbers. Dollars and cents are easy to measure, but so what? These numbers represent the results of both good and bad decisions and their consequences.

Getting Serious About Closing the Gaps

I've said from the beginning that this book is intended to crack open the door so that you can begin to consider the five capitals of your business. It is not a definitive guide. In fact, there is no *Success in Business Cookbook*. Every entrepreneur knows that people who are looking for the exact recipe for a perfect business structure should get nine-to-five jobs because they will never find the formula for running a business. Invariably, your business will have gaps. Just as there is no perfect life, there is no perfect business.

So how do you find the exact solutions? To start, more than a few books have been written about each of the capitals, so if you are a reader, read! The publisher of this book, Business Expert Press, for example, has published volumes of analysis and advice authored by some of the world's top educators and practitioners. You can start crafting solutions by visiting www.businessexpertpress.com and looking for additional resources.

The second way is to look externally to advisors.

Find the Right Advisors

I suggest that you start by looking at your social capital network and find a person who specializes in your needs, who knows you, your values, and your organization, and then pay that person to help you.

Taking your business to the next level is probably not something that can be accomplished through a generalized approach. Here, I am reminded of a friend whose two-year-old daughter cut open her eyebrow by falling from the couch and hitting the edge of the coffee table.

My friend texted a picture of the wound to her stepmom, a pediatric nurse, and asked, "Should I take her to the ER and get stitches for this?"

"Save yourself the time and the money," said my friend's stepmom. "That cut isn't very deep. The most they will do is glue it closed. Just stick a butterfly bandage on it, and give her some ice cream."

The wound did close on its own, eventually, but my friend's daughter, who is now four years old, has a nasty scar running through her eyebrow, one that could have been avoided if a microsurgeon had closed the gap above her eye. My friend made the mistake of asking someone who had general knowledge rather than the only expert who truly knew the answer: a pediatric plastic surgeon.

Add to Your Reading List

Getting advice that isn't tailored to your goals is like wearing shoes that are a little bit too big. They never quite feel right, and you constantly have to make adjustments. If you want to understand the importance of having advisors who discover and understand you and your goals first and foremost, read *Say Hello to the Elephants* by yours truly.

You can get plenty of advice on how to close the gaps in your business, but if you are truly committed to erasing them, my suggestion is that you find an expert in your network, and then pay that expert to help you find your solutions.

Find Your Pixie Dust

Looking externally to advisors will give you an important part of the solution. The true magic, though, comes by looking internally within your organization and finding the intersection of your human, social, intellectual, structural, and financial capital—that place where your organization really flies.

Dan Sullivan, master business strategist and founder of The Strategic Coach, coined the term *unique ability* to describe the confluence of an individual's talents and passion. Everyone has a unique ability. Its characteristics can be defined as follows:

1. A superior ability that other people notice and appreciate. They might say, "It blows my mind that you are so good at ____."
2. You are passionate about it, and you want to do it as much as possible.
3. It energizes you and those around you.
4. You keep getting better at it, and you never run out of possibilities to improve it or leverage it.

Written out like this, a person's unique ability might seem obvious. But some people spend their lives never truly pinpointing it. When they do find it, lightning strikes. As a 14-year student of Sullivan, I have sat in classrooms and watched countless of my fellow students find, and then leverage, their unique ability. When they do, they exhale in a deep sigh of relief.

This is what life is about, they think.

The same is true of an organization. When all the pieces come together, you can *feel* it—and so can your employees, vendors, clients, and colleagues. I call this pixie dust and it occurs when all five capitals meet in a perfect confluence. It is the reason your clients or customers turn to you—and only you. It is the reason your company is perceived as having more value than the competition.

So how do you find your pixie dust? Here are five questions that can get you started:

1. *Financial capital: What is realistic in the context of the money that is available to my firm?*
   Realistic. That might seem an odd word choice. After all, realistic is safe, boring, and probable.

   So to be clear: Think big. Think hairy. Think audacious.

   But when it comes to the money, be realistic. Too many entrepreneurs have fabulous ideas and great abilities but lack the financial resources to implement those ideas. They plan to take their business from 0 to 80 in 5 seconds.

   While this might happen for some companies, it isn't likely to happen for most.

   I look at it like this: If you have ever seen the Judy Garland and Mickey Rooney movies, you might remember a scene that looked something like this: They had a problem. They needed to raise money to solve this problem. So they decided to put on a show.

   Voila! As if by magic, the show would be produced. Elaborate set design that cost a fortune? Not a problem! Beautiful costumes? A huge orchestra? Not a problem!

   Is this real life? Not a chance!

   But it is with this same Hollywood grandeur that many entrepreneurs go forth. While I embrace big dreams and bold moves, right-sizing the expectations for capitalizing on pixie dust should be realistic and incremental.

   Building your pixie dust must be viewed as a process that works within the context of the monetary resources that are available. So have big ideas, but make sure that you can act on those big ideas by having sufficient resources to implement those ideas.

   If one starts a restaurant that is to serve only the best quality meat and produce, having a very small operating budget while the establishment cultivates a following is pretty unrealistic. The pricing per plate of the items on the menu is going to be higher than a normal restaurant. Your waste is liable to be very expensive waste. It takes time for customers to find the restaurant. Having a larger than normal operating capital reserve is required for such a venture.

2. *Intellectual capital: What is superior about my product, service, or company?*

   What do your clients say is different, unique, or superior about your intellectual capital? And let's be honest here about whether your intellectual capital truly is superior.

   Prior to the emergence of Uber and Lyft, a taxicab company might have said that its cars were cleaner, but this was not enough to dominate an industry. No one will ever be in awe of a clean car.

   If your product or service is lacking that wow factor that blows its competitors out of the water, ask a second question: *What can I do to strengthen my product or service so that it dominates its industry?*

   Cab companies who were looking for pixie dust would have known that their clients would be blown away if they had a tracking device that coupled as a real-time estimate of when the car would arrive, as well as an auto-payment option and a method of communicating with the driver.

   Cab companies were not looking for pixie dust, but Uber was.

   To be certain, you do *not* need to have unique intellectual capital to find your pixie dust. A standard product or service can be part of pixie dust, so long as it joins forces with the other four capitals in such a way that it creates magic and bonds a client with a company.

   Ask these questions nonetheless, and keep asking them over the years. As technology and the industry changes, you might or might not find that your pixie dust is becoming less and less powerful absent the addition of new intellectual capital.

3. *Human capital: When is my team really in the groove?*

   Think back to a time when you, your partners, and your employees really pulled together to meet a deadline or reach a goal. What conditions were present that allowed your team to band together?

   Now consider the answer to this in the context of your team's values, intelligences, and striving instincts.

When you know and can replicate the conditions that must be met for your team to produce, you can create that magical in the groove feeling with your team. Indeed, the application of top values, as well as your allegiance to the attributes and motivators of your team members, creates the condition for your team to click.

4. *Social capital: If my product or service was dominating its industry, who are the people or groups who would be using it, promoting it, and supporting it?*
When you find a way to reach and become sticky with these people or groups, you will have part of the formula for pixie dust.

Think back to the taxicab example. Taxicabs need the support of hotels, airports, business people, travelers, and late-night drinkers. And while taxicabs certainly had the market share, this was due only to a lack of competition. Perhaps the staff at the hotel, club, or restaurant received and appreciated tips by cab companies, but few—if any—companies or customers felt deeply bonded to any one taxi service. Most riders were burdened by their taxi service and felt inconvenienced by the need to call a cab, wait for its arrival, and then suffer the jarring and often unpleasant ride.

Compare this to Uber, which has a loyal band of users who rave about its service, promote it to friends, and wouldn't dream of taking a taxi.

This is what it means to become sticky.

5. *Structural capital: If I had an integrated process in place to make sure that my company was constantly evaluating, improving, and leveraging its social, human, intellectual, and financial capital, what would that process look like?*
Disney's Pixar Animation Studios uses a unique structure called the Braintrust to provide feedback to directors during the filmmaking process. Unlike most committees charged with providing feedback on a project, the Braintrust has absolutely no authority over the director. The director can take or leave the constructive criticism and suggestions, many of which are major.

In an article published in *Fast Company* magazine, Pixar's president, Ed Catmull, explained why this is an essential component of Pixar's process. "The Braintrust's notes, then, are intended to bring the true causes of problems to the surface—not to demand a specific remedy."

So instead of having to deal solely with studio heads, who are making demands independent of the creative process and focused more exclusively on the bottom line, Pixar's directors get creative feedback from creative-types that is intended to spark their own artistic resourcefulness.

Although Disney's Pixar has a creative process much larger and more complex than the Braintrust, this is the type of structural capital that helps a company find its pixie dust.

(And I suspect Disney knows something about finding pixie dust.)

Critical to this process is finding the right people to sit in the right spots. Pixar asks people intimately familiar with the storytelling process to sit on the Braintrust. Heads of studios, also known as Suits, are invited only if they also have a knack for storytelling. This is likely because the Suits are typically charged with making sure the movie performs in the box office, regardless of whether story is compromised in the process. They are bottom-line guys and gals, and they may or may not be creative types.

So when considering the best structure, also ask yourself who should sit in which seats within this process. A high-functioning company can create a structure for putting a group of people, each with their own pixie dust, in the right seats for delivering the best possible product or service to its constituents. If you are a Suit, you might need creative types who can develop your intellectual capital, brainstorming initially without your financial worries about cost-effectiveness being part of the process.

A Word About Precision

The truth is that even by asking externally and looking internally, the process of finding your pixie dust isn't as precise as you might want.

Many people emotionally or conatively seek precision before they are able to move. Some entrepreneurs, on the other hand, tend to move on a whim. Both of these groups are wrong, and both of them are right.

Any business's progress is based upon sets of assumption about the future. So many things affect the future—the global economy, new innovation, politics, and the like—that any move by the business is never likely to create the exact result intended.

Initially, a business's behaviors will result in some unexpected results, some of which might be good and some of which might be bad. That does not mean that you should never make a move. What it means rather is: Be thoughtful about what results can be expected, and then measure the actual against that expected.

Once measured, the next set of predictions is likely to be closer to the target if those predictions are predicated on the new information gleaned from the past results. It is like refining a site on a gun. Finding your pixie dust is about some trial and error, but it is based on good and reliable feedback.

And once you do find it, your pixie dust will allow your company to fly.

(Consider yourself lucky that I saved the corny one-liner until the very end of this book!)

Notes

Introduction

1. The stories in this book are based on people and businesses I know, but many of the details have been changed to protect the confidentiality of my social capital constituents.

Chapter 1

1. EOS is a company of advisors—which they call "EOS Implementers"—who take their clients through a refined process that helps them identify their competencies, best opportunities, and processes for sustained and rewarding growth and process.
2. I stole this saying from my partner Eric Swenson. Who knows where he stole it from?

Chapter 2

1. In *Say Hello to the Elephants*, I explain that self-orientation is one of the four parts of a formula that can be used to evaluate and rate an advisor.

Bibliography

Aron. September 14, 2011. "Being a Lululemon Ambassador," http://www .runnersrambles.com/2011/09/being-a-lululemon-ambassador.html.

Berniker, M.; and J. Lipton. November 6, 2013. "Uber CEO Kalanick: No Plans to Go Public Now." *CNBC.com.*

Catmull, Ed. April 2014. "Inside the Pixar Braintrust." *Fast Company.*

Chansanchai, A. July 13, 2011. "Outrage Over Netflix Rate Hike Continues." *Today Tech.*

Chen, B. July 1, 2012. "Uber, an App That Summons a Car, Plans a Cheaper Service Using Hybrids." *The New York Times.*

Cohan, P. June 17, 2013. "Four Lessons Amazon Learned From Webvan's Flop." *Forbes.*

Cohan, P. May 24, 2010. "Growth Matters: FreshDirect Nudges Its Way to Profits." *Daily Finance.*

Dumas, C.R. May 31, 2013. "Chobani: Culture Ripe for Growth." *Capital Press.*

Durisin, M. May 3, 2013. "Chobani CEO: Our Success Has Nothing to do With Yogurt." *Business Insider.*

Eastman Kodak Company. Case No. 12-10202 (ALG). United States Bankruptcy Court, Southern District of New York.

Elmer-DeWitt, P. October 2, 2013. "How Apple Became the World's Most Valuable Brand." *CNNMoney.*

Gardner, H. 2006. *Multiple Intelligences: New Horizons in Theory and Practice.* New York, NY: Basic Books.

Green, N. July 4, 2012. "AEG Purchases South Coast Soccer City Facility in Torrance." *Daily Breeze.*

Heffernan, M. 2011. *Willful Blindness: Why We Ignore the Obvious at Our Peril.* New York, NY: Walker & Company.

Helliker, K. September 13, 2010. "Lululemon Grows Fast on Slim Budget." *Wall Street Journal.*

Idrees, Y. February 12, 2013. "Can Sony Get Back the 'Wow.'" *The Motley Fool.*

Interbrand. 2013. "Best Global Brands 2013: Sony." Interbrand's 2013 report, http://www.interbrand.com/en/best-global-brands/2013/Sony (accessed May 12, 2014).

Jeffers, G. 2013. "Global Attractions Attendance Report." *Themed Entertainment Association.*

Lululemon Athletica Corporation. 2013 "Lululemon Athletica Inc Form 10-K." *Lululemon Athletica Corporation*, http://files.shareholder.com/downloads/LULU/3117955639x0x677637/64A2CB6B-0B78-41FD-A536-B99C8245F022/2012_Annual_Report.pdf (accessed May 7, 2014).

Lunce, S.E.; L.M. Lunce; Kawai, Y.; and B. Maniam. 2006. "Success and Failure of Pure-play Organizations: Webvan versus Peapod, a Comparative Analysis." *Industrial Management and Data Systems* 106, no. 9, pp. 1344–1358.

Maheshwani, S. July 16, 2012. "Gap Athleta Stalks Lululemon One Yoga Store at a Time." Bloomberg.com.

Mcardle, M. April 2, 2012. "Why You Can't Get a Taxi." *The Atlantic*.

Merrefield, D. June 5, 2012. "Online-Based Grocery Delivery Thrives At Last." *The Robin Report*.

Pai, A. July 9, 2013. "L.A., Let Uber's Cars Share the Road." *Los Angeles Times*.

Potter, N. September 19, 2011. "Netflix CEO Apologizes for Price Increase, Announces Qwikster Service to Mail DVDs." *ABC News.com*.

PR Newswire. April 26, 2013. "Chobani CEO Honored as Disruptive Innovator at Tribeca Disruptive Innovation Awards." *PR Newswire*.

PR Newswire. April 19, 2013. "Chobani's New Twin Falls, Idaho Plant Named 'Plant of the Year' by Food Engineering." *PR Newswire*.

Rogers, S. July 12, 2013. "When a #Sharknado Attacks!" *Twitter*.

Rose, T. 2008. *Say Hello to the Elephants: A Four-Part Process for Finding Clarity, Confronting Problems, and Moving On*. Los Angeles: RSJ/Swenson LLC.

Rusli, E.M. April 9, 2012. "Facebook Buys Instagram for $1 Billion." *New York Times*.

Sandoval, G. July 11, 2012. "Netflix's Lost Year: The Inside Story of the Price-Hike Train Wreck." *CNET News*.

Stewart, J.B. April 26, 2013. "Netflix Chief Looks Back on Its Near-Death Spiral." *The New York Times*.

Tabuchi, H. April 14, 2012. "How the Tech Parade Passed Sony." *The New York Times*.

Thomas, B. 1976. *Walt Disney, An American Original*. New York, NY: Simon and Schuster.

Tran-ecommerce. 2011 "Why did Webvan fail so spectacularly," http://tran-ecommerce.blogspot.com/2011/01/webvan.html (accessed May 7, 2014).

Tsotsis, A. June 2, 2012. "For Limo Service Uber, Downtime and Idle Resources Are Fuel for Profits." *Wired*.

Wickman, G. 2011. *Traction: Get a Grip on Your Business*. Dallas: BenBella Books.

World Class Benchmarking. n.d. "Disney's Four Keys to a Great Guest Experience," *World Class Benchmarking*, http://worldclassbenchmarking.com/disneys-four-keys-to-a-great-guest-experience (accessed May 7, 2014).

Zax, D. October 11, 2011. "Netflix's Qwikster Debacle." *MIT Technology Review*.

Index

OTHER TITLES IN THE ENTREPRENEURSHIP AND SMALL BUSINESS MANAGEMENT COLLECTION

Scott Shane, Case Western University, Editor

- *Growing Your Business: Making Human Resources Work for You* by Robert Baron
- *Managing Your Intellectual Property Assets* by Scott Shane
- *Internet Marketing for Entrepreneurs: Using Web 2.0 Strategies for Success* by Susan Payton
- *Business Plan Project: A Step-by-Step Guide to Writing a Business Plan* by David Sellars
- *Sales and Market Forecasting for Entrepreneurs* by Tim Berry
- *Strategic Planning: Fundamentals for Small Business* by Gary May
- *Starting Your Business* by Sanjyot Dunung
- *Growing Your Business* by Sanjyot Dunung
- *Understanding the Family Business* by Keanon J. Alderson
- *Launching a Business: The First 100 Days* by Bruce Barringer
- *The Manager's Guide to Building a Successful Business* by Gary W. Randazzo
- *Social Entrepreneurship: From Issue to Viable Plan* by Terri D. Barreiro and Melissa M. Stone
- *Healthcare Entrepreneurship* by Rubin Pillay
- *The Successful Management of Your Small Business: A Focus on Planning, Marketing, and Finance* by Pat Roberson-Saunders
- *The Chinese Entrepreneurship Way: A Case Study Approach* by Julia Pérez-Cerezo
- *Enhancing the Managerial DNA of Your Small Business* by Pat Roberson-Saunders, Barron H. Harvey, Philip Fanara, Jr., Gwynette P. Lacy and Pravat Choudhury

Announcing the Business Expert Press Digital Library

Concise E-books Business Students Need for Classroom and Research

This book can also be purchased in an e-book collection by your library as
- a one-time purchase,
- that is owned forever,
- allows for simultaneous readers,
- has no restrictions on printing, and
- can be downloaded as PDFs from within the library community.

Our digital library collections are a great solution to beat the rising cost of textbooks. E-books can be loaded into their course management systems or onto students' e-book readers.

The **Business Expert Press** digital libraries are very affordable, with no obligation to buy in future years. For more information, please visit **www.businessexpertpress.com/librarians**. To set up a trial in the United States, please email **sales@businessexpertpress.com**.

www.ingramcontent.com/pod-product-compliance
Lightning Source LLC
Chambersburg PA
CBHW062034200326
41519CB00017B/5038